DATE DUE			
Mar 18 '80			
Dec 12 '80			

Gymnastics for Girls and Women

Randi Norman
Oslo, Norway

WM. C. BROWN COMPANY PUBLISHERS
135 SOUTH LOCUST STREET • DUBUQUE, IOWA 52003

Manufactured by WM. C. BROWN CO. INC., Dubuque, Iowa
Printed in U. S. A.

Preface

On request, I have revised and translated my book into English. It contains exercises and gymnastics (arranged in programs), materials for tumbling, balance beam, and some of the most used vaultings over buck, box and horse. The apparatus work in the programs are only suggestions, indicating how to work in groups. This book may serve as a textbook for teachers in junior high schools (the first ten programs), senior high schools, colleges, teacher training institutions, and universities. I hope it will be of some help to physical education students at all levels.

This book also contains two programs (lessons) which were used in a demonstration with physical education students at Washburn University, Topeka, Kansas. The idea was to show how to make up a demonstration from exercises used in daily lessons.

It will be of considerable aid if a pianist is available to accompany the exercises. It should be music with a good regular cadence to fit the tempo of the exercises.

I am much obliged to Helen M. Hocker of the Physical Education Department at Washburn University for her interest in my work and the great help she has rendered in making possible this American version, and to Janet Nuzman, also of Washburn University, who assisted Miss Hocker with the editing of the manuscript.

Randi Norman

Oslo, Norway
May, 1965

Introduction

Mrs. Randi Norman was a visiting Fulbright lecturer at Washburn University during the 1963 Spring semester. We found her an enthusiastic and highly competent teacher. She shared all of her talents freely not only in our school but also in local public schools and recreation agencies, as well as in other colleges and universities in Kansas.

Mrs. Norman is a teacher in Valler Secondary School in a suburb of Oslo, Norway. She also has charge of the student gymnastic club at the University of Oslo and is a member of the faculty of the University of Oslo International Summer School. She is widely recognized as one of the experts in gymnastics in Scandinavia; and, as a student at the Physical Education Academy, she was a member of the Norwegian Women's Gymnastic team which performed in the Olympics in Berlin in 1936. She now conducts gymnastic institutes for teachers and students all over Norway and in many parts of Europe.

From these many contacts have come requests for her book *Gymnastic Tabeler For Jenter* to be translated into English. I feel confident this revised edition of the book, which is widely used as a text in both Denmark and Norway, will be of great value to both secondary teachers and those who are in professional preparation in our colleges and universities.

We have taken the liberty of changing a few words to conform to our way of expression and for the sake of clarity; however, we have retained most of the original translation because it often expresses the action in a charming manner.

It is a great pleasure to present this American version of *Norwegian Gymnastic Programs For Girls and Women.*

Helen M. Hocker

Washburn University
Topeka, Kansas

Use of the Material

The material in this book is presented in a series of progressive lessons (programs) as performed in Norwegian classes. When using this material, however, teachers in our country may choose to adapt it to their own classes and situations. Although the exercises are used to strengthen the body for movement, they are done with precision and exactness. Teachers will, of course, adapt the number of times that an exercise is performed to the ability level of their groups. When good form is developed and the class is well conditioned, the degree of repetition of each exercise may well be limited to a group routine of five to ten minutes. These routines, when done to music, not only serve as enjoyable conditioning exercises for classes but also are easily adaptable for demonstrations (see Section C).

An explanation of a few terms used in the manuscript is given in footnotes which appear within the body of the text. The book is divided into seven sections: floor exercises; mat work and tumbling; rhythm ball exercises; balance beam; and vaulting on buck, horse and vaulting box. There are twenty lessons in the floor exercise section which are graded in difficultly. In the gymnastic and floor exercise section additional supplemental material is also included. Suggestions are then made regarding how this material can be used for demonstration programs.

(HMH – JN)

Table of Contents

Mrs. Randi Norman with students from Washburn University, Topeka, Kansas, where she was a visiting Fulbright lecturer in 1962

Graded Programs

PROGRAM I

Formation: in files, in closed formation. . . . . .

1. Walking, running (in place)

Stand on the left foot. Right big toe meets the floor, stretched ankle. Take the opposite position, stand on the right foot, etc. Make the change without raising the toe from the floor. Pass on to raising the knee higher. Run forward.

Walking

Put your left foot forward, the heel only touching the floor. Move on by rolling from the distal part of the heel the toes pointing straight forward. Keep the weight on the front foot while pushing with the right big toe. Arms and shoulders relaxed, look fairly upwards. Walk out in four rays[1] from the middle of the gymnasium.

2. Jump

Jumping on the spot, hips, knees and ankles stretched while leaving the floor; land on the toes, go down on full foot, and continue (Count 1-2).

3. Arm exercise

Standing position, feet together, small relaxed arm swings, forward, backward. Repeat with genuflection[2] (Count 1-2). Palms turned backward. Then swing all the way forward up to tall standing position, arms extended overhead. From this position stretch alternately left and right reaching upward. Then drop the arms relaxed, down. Repeat exercise.

4. Leg exercise

(a) Standing, feet together. Place the left foot a short step forward, stand on tiptoes, small kneebending and stretching (Count 1-2), deep bending and stretching (Count 3-4). The same with right foot moving forward, etc.

(b) Squat position, arms stretched forward, shoulder distance apart. "Hare-jumping" on the spot. Put both hands on the floor, just in front of the knees, keep shoulder distance between the hands. Kick up to squat hand stand with bent knees and try to get hips and back perpendicular to floor (Count: up and down).

(c) Hare-jumps moving forward and backward.

---

[1]Rays — lines — JN.
[2]Genuflection — knees slightly flexed and extended — JN.

5. **Back exercise**

   Standing position, bend the upper part of the back backward (Count 1-2), stretch to starting position (Count 3-4). The head starts and ends the bending. Do not tighten the shoulderblades. Keep weight forward on feet so that lower back does not bob.

6. **Back exercise**

   Standing position, hands held loosely on the lower back. Bend forward from the hips, keeping the back a little arched, look forward (Count 1-2), stretch to starting position (Count 3-4). Repeat several times. Stop in the angle-position for control. Then relax arms, neck, back, and knees, back rounded, head down. Roll the back up to standing position (piece by piece).[3]

7. **Hop**

   Standing position. Two hops on right foot (use the ankle), swing left leg to the left, approximately 45 degrees. Repeat on left foot, swing right leg to the right.

8. **Leg exercise**

   Standing position, feet apart, the toes pointing at an angle of approximately 45 degrees. Bend left knee, raise left heel a little (keep the back straight). (The center of gravity is thus moved a little to the left.) Back to starting position (Count 3-4). Repeat to the right (Count 1-2, 3-4). Bend the knee more each time.

9. **Abdominal exercise**

   (a) Lying on the back, arms relaxed along the sides, bend both knees (keep the whole back on the floor) (Count 1-2). Stretch both legs slowly upward (Count 3-4), bend the knees, the legs falling relaxed down. (Count 5-6), sliding to starting position (Count 7-8). Repeat several times. Last time move the stretched legs backward touching the floor behind the head. Move the leg slowly down to starting position. Roll down the back first, then the legs afterward. If difficulties occur in keeping the back on floor during the last part of the exercise, raise the head and look at the feet.

---

[3]Gradually straighten spine from lower back to neck with head rising last — JN.

(b) Lying on the back, raise the hips to "build a bridge" with the lower part of the back (Count 1-2). Lower the hips down by using the abdominal muscles, press the back against the floor (Count 3-4).

10. Abdominal exercise

Lying on the back, bend knees to the right, raise to knee-standing position, turning 90 degrees to the right (Count 1-2), sit down on the left side and lie down turning 90 degrees once more. Do not use the hands. Stop in knee-standing position.

11. Side exercise

Knee-standing position. Bend straight to the left, arms and neck relaxed (the head hanging against the shoulder) (Count 1-2). Stretch to starting position (Count 3-4). Start stretching from the waistline. Repeat to the right side. When finished, place hands on the floor and raise to standing position with a jump.

12. Skip

Skip forward on tiptoe making small knee-bendings, arms swinging relaxed from the shoulders. Stress the foot work. To the stallbar. If such is not available, work in couples.

13. Leg, hip exercise

Standing with the right side to the wall, right hand on wall or grasping stallbar. Swing left leg forward and backward from the hip. Relax the leg, keep the knee a little bent all the time, touch the floor on every swing.

14. Abdominal exercise

Sit on the floor, facing the stallbar with the feet under the lowest bar. Knees bent. Bend backward from

the hips, drop the head backward, arch the back a little (Count 1-2), back to starting position (Count 3-4). Go further down each time and try to reach the floor. The head starts the movement and gets up the last. (If desired work in couples, one standing on the knees holding the other's feet on the floor.)

15. Stretching exercise for hamstrings

Sitting on the floor, facing the wall, feet against the lowest bar, back straight up, arms extended forward shoulder-high. Lean forward from the hips, try to catch the third or fourth bar, small stretchings forward, smoothly, not staccato. Shake the legs. (If no stallbars — work with couples — facing with feet together — stretch and touch floor as far as possible.)

APPARATUS WORK

1st and 2nd week

Horizontal bar

(a) Adjust bar a little higher than the girls can reach standing on tiptoe. Standing under the bar, jump to hanging position, drop down, landing on the toes, bending ankles and knees not too deep, only halfway down.

(b) The bar chest high, hands on the bar. Jump up to front rest support position, the bar under the hips, stretched arms, back arched, legs stretched backward. Bend the back forward and move round the bar landing in starting position. Three girls working together, two helping each holding one hand on the hands of the performer, and the other catching under the performer's bent knees so that she does not reach the floor too abruptly. The spotters are standing on the opposite side of the bar.

Mat work

Forward roll, free form, see "Tumbling": forward roll. Get up with the hands around the knees. Later: finish with a high jump, swinging both arms forward and upward.

Take-off. Springboard training

Appliances: Springboard with a mat behind. Short slow run, last step on floor approximately one yard from the springboard (depending on the speed and the size of the performer). Low jump while swinging both arms backward, landing on the toes on the springboard — and jump straight up in the air, swinging the arms fast forward, upward, stretching ankles, knees and hips, land on the mat with slightly bent knees.

Balance beam

(a) Walking from one end of the beam to the other, jump down to the side.

(b) As (a), but walking on tiptoe.

3rd and 4th week

Balance beam

(a) Repeat from 1st and 2nd week.

(b) Running with small steps on tiptoe from one end of the beam to the other.

Mat work

(a) Forward roll, stress a good performance. Move the hands slightly forward, stretch the knees while rolling, finish with a high jump.

(b) One forward roll with stretched knees, two hare-jumps forward.

Ropes

Each girl 2 ropes, 3 working together. The girl standing between the ropes holds one rope in each hand, eye height. Swing the legs forward up with bent knees and turn round till the feet reach the floor on the opposite side, then tuck head in, bending your knees go back to starting position. The spotters cover her hands with one hand and help her to get around with the other.

Buck

Stress the running and take off, jump over the buck with legs wide apart. Two spotters standing on the "landing" side of the buck, catching her upper part of the arm and holding her until she is in balance on the mat.

PROGRAM II

1. **Walking, running**

   March to the places in four lines. Walking in place, roll on the feet, stretch the ankles. Pass on to running in place; stress the foot-work. Move forward and backwards in short steps.

2. **Arm exercise**

   (a) Standing position, arm swing forwards and backwards with small knee bendings (Count 1-2), arm swing forward, upwards (Count 3). Arms falling forwards, down, a little backwards, knee dipping (Count 4). Stretch as far as possible on Count 3. Repeat several times.

   (b) The same as (a), adding relaxation and stretching of the back in every arm swing.

3. **Leg exercise**

   Standing in couples, side by side, join inner hands. Leg swings forwards (outside leg) (Count 1), backwards (Count 2), forwards (Count 3). Closed feet, 90 degree turn, facing partner, join hands, stand on tiptoe (Count 4). Bend the knees half way down, stretch (Count 5-6) bend the knees deep to squat position, stretch with 90 degree turn the opposite way (Count 7-8). Repeat beginning on other leg.

4. **Back exercise**

   On the knees, sitting on the heels, arms extended forward. Bend the upper back backwards with left arm raised upwards (Count 1-2), stretch to starting position (Count 3-4). Repeat with raising the right arm. The head starts and ends the bending.

5. **Back — foot exercise**

   On hands and knees, ankles extended. Raise the hips high, stretch knees and ankles, raise on the toe-nails (Count 1-2), bend to starting position (Count 3-4).

6. **Hops**

   (a) Skip forward in small hops, one on each foot, stretched ankles, knee slightly bent.

   (b) As (a) moving backwards.

   (c) Four hops forward as (a). Four jumps on the spot, closed feet

8

(Count 1-8), four hops backwards as (b). Four jumps on the spot with closed feet (Count 1-8).

7. Leg exercise

Standing position, a long step to the left on left foot, land on the toes, knee bent (Count 1), bend the knee deeper (Count 2), push with the left foot, stretch knee and ankle (Count 3) to starting position (Count 4). Repeat to the right side. (See Program I, Exercise 8.)

8. Back exercise

(a) Standing with the back bent forward down from the hips, arms extended far forward against the floor. Alternate stretching farther forward, left and right side and arm.

(b) Relax neck, arms, back, and knees. Small knee dippings. Roll the back to starting position. (See Program I, Exercise 6.)

9. Side exercise

Standing position arms at side, bend to the left, relax head, knees and arms; two dippings with further bending (Count 1-3), stretch from the waistline. (4) Repeat to the right.

10. Running exercise

Standing position, three running steps in place, left, right, left foot (Count 1, 2, 3) hop on the left foot, raise the right knee (Count 4). Repeat right, left, right, raise left knee, etc. Stress the footwork.

11. Balance

In couples, join inner hands, left leg extended backwards, toes on the floor, stretched knee and ankle. Raise left leg backwards from the hip, keep the back straight up (Count 1-2), down (Count 3-4). Several times. Repeat with the right leg.

12. Back exercise

Lying on the stomach, hands on the floor, by the shoulders, fingers pointing forward. B e n d backwards, stretch the arms, start with the head and upper back, try to look at the wall behind. Keep the hips to the floor if possible (Count 1-4). Back to starting position (Count 5-8), relax the legs, toes together, heels apart.

13. **Abdominal exercise**

Lying on the back, arms relaxed along the sides of the body. Move stretched legs upwards, toes touching the floor behind the head (Count 1-4), lower the legs to starting position. Roll the back down first, then the legs. (See Program I, Exercise 9.)

14. **Dancing steps**

Three steps forward, left, right, left, the middle one short. A small hop on the left foot, raise right leg with a little knee bending and stretched ankle, moving the leg approximately 45 degrees to the left. (Count 1-2-3-4.) Repeat forward, right, left, right, hop, raise left leg, etc. The body and the arms follow the movement, look at the foot.

Walking to the stallbar or to the wall.

15. **Leg, hip exercise**

Standing position, right side to the wall, right hand on the wall, left foot behind the right, left foot toes turned to the left. Swing left leg to the side as high as possible and down to starting position (Count 1-2). Several times with left leg, turn and repeat with the right leg.

16. **Handstand**

First step to learning the handstand. (See "Tumbling": Handstand (a).)

APPARATUS WORK

1st and 2nd week

Bar

(a) The bar a little higher than the girls can reach standing on tiptoe, Jump up (See Program I) move sideways to the other end of the bar by transferring alternately left and right hand, jump down correctly. (On toes first — JN.)

(b) Repeat the movement to the other side.

Mat work

(a) Several rolls forward (stretched knees or Pike) in succession. Finish with a high jump.

(b) Start the backward roll.

Balance beam

(a) Walking backward.
(b) As (a), on tiptoe.

Girls in classes at Real Secondary School, Valler, Norway

Vaulting box

(a) Crosswise, approximately chest high or a little lower.[4] Running, take-off, jump on the box in squat position, jump farther forward and off the box. Two spotters assist by grasping under arms of vaulter.

(b) As (a), jump over the box.

3rd and 4th week

Balance beam

(a) Repeat the walking and running from Program I.
(b) Skip. Move forward in small jumps (See Program I, Exercise 12).

Mat work

(a) Repeat the walking forward and backward roll from Programs I and II.
(b) Several backward rolls in succession.
(c) Two backward rolls, two backward hare-jumps.[5]

Ropes

(a) Repeat the hand-spring backwards and forwards as in Program I.
(b) Build "a swallow's nest." Fasten one foot to each rope, just over the hands, lower the hips, raise the head, arch the back.

Vaulting buck

The buck a little higher than last time. Put the hands on the end of the buck close to the springboard, short touch, look up and stretch. 2 spotters.

---

[4] 43 inches high corresponds to side horse height — JN.
[5] Execute as in forward hare-jumps only extend legs backward after momentary balance — JN.

PROGRAM III

1. Walking, running

Four heavy steps on full foot, relaxed neck, back and arms (Count 1-8). Two counts on each step. Eight light, running steps on tiptoe (Count 1-8).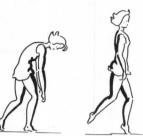

2. Arm exercise

Standing position, left arm extended to the side shoulder height. Relax left arm swinging it down and across in front of the body, relaxed knees and central back (Count 1). Swing left arm out to starting position dipping and stretching knees and back (Count 2). Several times with left arm. Repeat with the right.

3. Leg exercise

Standing in couples, join inner hands. Swing left leg forward, backward, forward (Count 1-3) bend right knee and stretch, touch the floor with left big toe (Count 4).[6] Step forward on left foot, swing right leg, etc. (Count 1-4.)

4. Leg exercise (fun)

In couples facing each other join hands, one sitting on the floor with bent knees, the other standing, leaning backwards. The one stretches slowly to standing position while the other bends to sitting position. Count: 1-4. Continue changing. "Weighing salt."

5. Jumping

(a) Standing position. Hop on the right foot, place left heel on the floor in front, a little to the left (Count 1), hop on right foot, stretch left ankle and touch the floor with the toes (Count 2), two jumps in place with closed feet (Count 3-4). Repeat with the right foot, hopping on the left (Count 5-8).

(b) Standing position. Four slides sideways to the left (Count 1-4), four jumps on the spot, closed feet (Count 5-8). Repeat to the right.

(c) Combine (a) and (b), (a) Count 1-8, (b) Count 1-8, then start with the opposite foot Count 1-8, 1-8.

---

[6]Left leg should be extended, 4″ − 6″ above floor and right knee must bend in order to touch left toes to floor − JN.

6. Back exercise

Standing position, alternate arm swing forward, backward. Left arm forward, right arm backward (Count 1). Change (Count 2), swing left arm up (Count 3), bend backward (upper back) (Count 4). Left arm falls forward, down, backward, right arm forward (Count 1), change (Count 2). Swing right arm up (Count 3), etc. All the time relaxing and stretching knees and back.

7. Back exercise

Standing position, arms swing forward to shoulder height with knee dipping and stretching (Count 1). Bend forward from the hips and stretch forward as far as possible touching the floor, two times (Count 2-3). After Count 3 stretch to standing position with the arms extended forward. Then let the arms fall forward down and a little backward, relaxed knees and back (Count 4). Repeat several times. Stop in position and stretch farther forward, alternately left and right side and arm. Relax neck, back, arms, and knees, roll up to standing position. (See Program II, Exercise 8.)

8. Abdominal, leg, and back exercise

(a) Standing on the knees, arms relaxed along the sides. Lean backwards from the knees, the back a little arched (Count 1-3), to starting position (Count 4-6).

(b) "Horseback riding." Sitting on the heels, arms extended forward. Move the hips from heels up and down as sitting on a running horse. Try to push the hips forward every time.

9. Side exercise

Standing on the knees, arms extended upward, bend forward and turn to the left, place the hands on the floor on the outside of the left leg three times while moving the hips up and down (Count 1-3), stretch to starting position, making a big circle with the arms sideways and up (Count 4). Repeat to the opposite side.

10. Jump

Standing position. Three jumps on the spot, closed feet (Count 1-3), one high jump with the legs apart (Count 4).

11. Leg exercise

(a) Standing on the right foot, left leg extended backwards from the hip, toes touching the floor, knee and ankle extended. Raise left leg from hip. Keep the back straight up (Count 1-2). Return to starting position (Count 3-4). Repeat with right leg (Count 5-8). (See Program II, Exercise 11.)

(b) Raise the leg higher while moving the upper body forward and downward with arched back, toward front scale.

12. Back — abdominal exercise

Sitting on the floor, legs extended, arms extended upwards. Bend forward, bend the arms and stretch forward along the sides of the body (Count 1). Raise the back and arms forward up to starting position (Count 2-3), lean a little backwards with back straight (Count 4). Start next time from position 4.

13. Abdominal exercise

Lying on the back, left knee bent, right leg extended upwards. "Cycling." After awhile roll up on the neck, elbows on the floor, hands on the hip. Move down again and lower the legs close to the floor, keep on cycling. Relax. Try every time to bend and stretch the ankles as well.

14. Foot exercise

Lying on the back, knees bent, feet on the floor, toes together, heels apart. Raise heels, stretch the ankles, up on the big toe (Count 1-2), down to starting position, relax (Count 3-4). When finishing the exercise shake the legs, one at a time extended upwards.

15. Side exercise

Standing position, right arm extended upward. Bend to the left, relax knees, right arm and neck (Count 1). Bounce farther while flexing knees (Count 2-3), stretch from the waistline to starting position. Several times to the left. Repeat to the right.

16. Running steps

One high leaping step forward onto left foot (Count 1), two running steps, right, left (Count 2-3). Leap onto the right foot, two running steps, etc. Mazurka rhythm.

17. Leg, hip exercise

Standing with the right side to the stallbar (wall), the right hand on the bar or wall. Swing left leg from the hip, backwards, to the sides and forward in a big half circle. Repeat with the right leg.

18. Handstand

Starting position by the wall. See "Tumbling": handstand. Swing the back leg up, touch the wall, the other leg is hanging relaxed. (Count "up and down.")

APPARATUS WORK

1st and 2nd week

Bar

Chesthigh. Run, jump on the bar. (See Program I, 1st and 2nd week, bar (b).) Bend forward around the bar, round back, keep stretched knees, land at the same side as you start.

Mat work

Start the headstand with bent knees, see "Tumbling," headstand. One spotter.

Vaulting box

The box crosswise. Training jump over the box in squat position, stretch the knees and hips after clearing box and land on the mat with knees slightly flexed, arms extended out, a little up. Full balance.

Balance beam

Walk to the middle of the beam, swing one leg forward, standing foot on tiptoe, turn 180 degrees, walk backwards to the other end of the beam. Next time, swing the other leg and turn the opposite way.

3rd and 4th week

Balance beam

Waltzing steps on tiptoe from one end of the beam to the other.

Mat work

(a) More headstand training with bent knees — (tri-pod) — JN.
(b) Little by little, try to stretch the knees and hips. One spotter with one arm supporting the back of the performer. (Do not touch unless necessary.)

Ropes

Practice the tumbling and the "swallows nest" between two ropes (See Program I, 3rd and 4th week: ropes, as well as Program II, 3rd and 4th week: ropes). Try to stretch out hanging between the ropes with head down. Stretched knees all the time, bend only the hips.

Buck

(a) Continue to practice jumping over the buck.
(b) Turn the buck crosswise so that the girls have to get their legs wide apart when passing and only a short touch with the hands.

PROGRAM IV

1. Short time free practice, tumbling, handstand to the wall, ropes, balance beam, etc.

2. **Running**

   Run in one line around the gymnasium, then into four-line formation.

3. **Arm exercise**

   Standing position, feet together, arms swing forward, backwards, knee and back relaxing and stretching (Count 1-2), arms swing forward, up, all the way round in a big circle two times, knees and back relaxing and stretching (Count 3-4).[7]

4. **Leg exercise**

   Standing position, swing left leg forward, bend and stretch right knee (Count 1), bend and stretch right knee, touch the floor with the left foot toes (Count 2). Three steps forward in waltz rhythm (long, short, long). Stand on left foot, right foot extended backwards, a little above the floor. Repeat with the right leg forward (Count 5-8).

5. **Back exercise**

   Standing, feet together, weight forward, arms extended forward, shoulder distance apart. Move left arm forward up while bending upper back backwards (Count 1), two smooth, deeper bendings (only contract the long back muscles) (Count 2-3), stretch up, lower the arm to starting position (Count 4). Repeat raising right arm, etc. (Count 5-8). (See the same bending of the knees Program II, Exercise 4.)

6. **Back exercise**

   Standing (the feet a little apart). Bend forward from the hips, arch the back, try to look at the ceiling (Count 1-4), relax neck, arms, back, and knees, (Count 5), roll up to starting position (Count 6-8). (See Program I, Exercise 6.)

7. **Jump**

   Three running steps to the left, right foot crossing in front, (Count 1). Left foot to the side (Count 2), right foot crossing in front (Count 3). Jump on the right foot and swing left leg to the side approximately 45 degrees high (Count 4). Two hops on left foot, swing right leg to the side (Count 5-6). Two hops on right foot swinging the left leg to the side (Count 7-8). Repeat with the left leg crossing in front, moving to the right, etc., (Count 1-8).

---

[7]Stress that the entire body stretches as arms swing upward into full circle — JN.

8. **Side exercise**

Standing position, feet together, arms extended to the sides, shoulder high. Drop left arm relaxed along the side, raise right arm straight up, bend to the left, relax the knees, right arm hanging relaxed over the head (Count 1), two further bendings (Count 2-3), stretch to standing position, right arm moving up — down, left arm out to starting position (Count 4). Repeat the bending to the right side (Count 5-8). (See Program III, Exercise 15.)

9. **Abdominal, back exercise**

Stand on knees, arms relaxed along the sides. Lean backwards from the knees while twisting to the left, left arm moving in a low circle line to the side and backwards, touching the floor behind the left foot (Count 1-3), stretch to starting position (Count 4-6). Repeat to the right side (Count 1-3, 4-6). Look at the hand.

10. **Side exercise**

On the knees sitting on heels, turn continuously from one side to the other. Swing the arms relaxed from side to side around the body while bobbing up and down. (Raise seat from heels.)

11. **Jump**

Standing, two hops on right foot while bending left leg (foot behind the right knee, (1) stretching it to the side, and toward the floor (2), two jumps with closed feet (3-4). Repeat hop on the left foot (5-6), (7-8).

12. **Balance exercise**

Standing, left leg raising backwards from the hip (Count 1-2), left leg swinging down forward up (Count 3), to standing position with feet together (Count 4). Repeat (Count 5-6-7-8).

13. **Back exercise**

Lying on the stomach, hands on the floor, elbows bent, one hand over the other, the head on the hands. Stretch the arms forward up while bending the upper back backwards, head up (Count 1-4), to starting position, relax (Count 5-8). Watch the feet, the legs quite relaxed all the time, big toes together heels apart.

14. Foot exercise

Lying on the stomach (same starting position as Exercise 13) bend your knees, heels together, toes apart, keep the ankles bent. Flex the feet (try to make the foot as short as possible) (Count 1-2), stretch the feet, spread the toes (Count 3-4).

15. Back exercise

Sitting on the floor, legs extended straight back. Lean forward from the hips with the hands extended forward, one hand on each side of the legs on the floor (do not round the back), small stretching forward try to reach farther every time. Very small movements, keep the knees stretched.

16. Abdominal exercise

Long sitting (feet extended on floor in front of body), arms relaxed along the sides. Relax the center part of the back, piece by piece roll the back down to lying position, starting with the lower back (Count 1-4). Roll up to starting position, start with the head, rounded back (Count 5-7) and stretch the back (Count 8).

17. Side exercise

Sitting with bent knees, feet on the floor, right hand on left knee, left hand loosely over the right. Swing left arm in a large circle to the side and backwards, a little more than shoulder high, while turning the upper part  of the trunk to the left, look at hand (Count 1). Swing the arm immediately the same way back to starting position (Count 2). Several times without stop. Repeat to the right side.

18. Shoulder stretching exercise

Sitting with bent knees, feet on the floor, arms extended sideward a little more than shoulder high palms forward. Move the arms farther backwards with small stretchings (Count 1 and 2, etc.).

19. Dancing steps

Standing in large circle with couples facing each other, all moving in the same direction. Join right hands, keep the left hand on the hip. One step sideways with the left foot (Count 1), close the feet (Count 2), one step sideways with the left foot (Count 3), jump on the left foot while turning 180 degrees, swing the right leg down — forward, and swing the joined hands down — forward at the same time (Count 4). The girls are now standing back to back. (Count: *1-2-3*-jump.) *Continue with the right foot* (Count 4-5-6-8).

APPARATUS WORK

1st and 2nd week

Handstand

The whole group lined up facing the wall. Handstand starting position. Practice handstand all at the same time, one leg touching the wall, the other hanging relaxed. (Count up − − − and down.) Try to get the hips up.

Cartwheel

The group in zigzag by the wall (good distance between the two lines). Chalk up lines across the floor in front of each girl. Practice turning the cartwheel. See "Tumbling": Cartwheel (a), (b), (c).

3rd and 4th week

Balance beam

(a) Skip from one end of the beam to the other. In the beginning small jumps, slightly bent knees. Little by little higher jumps, raise the knee higher.

(b) Walk to the middle of the beam, standing on right foot arms extended forward, shoulder high, raise left leg backwards from the hip to front scale position (See Program II, Exercise 11). Repeat with the right leg. Walk to the end of the beam, jump down to the side, and come to standing position, hand resting on beam.

Tumbling

(a) Forward roll, get up on one foot, bent knee, the other leg and arms extended forwards.

(b) Practice cartwheel.

Vaulting box

Lengthwise. Jump to squat position at the nearest end of the box, hands on the box, forward roll, land on the mat with knees slightly bent, arms extended to the sides. 2 spotters along side at opposite end of box, to assist landing.

Ropes

(a) Free practice.
(b) Start climbing the ropes.

PROGRAM V

1. Walking, running

In one line, build a big circle, face the center of the circle.

2. Arm exercise

Standing position, arms extended upwards, look at the hands. Arms falling forward down, relax central back and knees. (Look forward all the time) (Count 1). Raise arms sideways up to starting position, stretch the whole body (Count 2-3).

3. Leg exercise

Bend the knees as deep as possible, keep the whole foot on floor, arms extended forward. Small movements further down, push the knees forward, try to get the hips down. Down — down! etc. Stretch up, shake legs and arms.

4. Back exercise

Face the center of the circle. On your knees, sit on heels, arms relaxed along the sides. Lean forward from the hips, look at the ceiling, arch the back, stretch the arms, palms down (Count 1-3), relax neck, back and arms (Count 4), roll the back up to start position (Count 5-6).

5. Side exercise

Hook sitting with feet on floor, right hand on left knee, left hand on the right. Twist to the left, swing left arm out, backwards shoulder high (Count 1). Two bounces farther backwards (Count 2-3), to starting position (Count 4). Repeat to the right side (Count 5-8).

6. Abdominal exercise

Sitting with bended knees, feet a little above the floor, stretched ankles, arms extended to the sides, fingertips on floor or shoulder high. Touch the floor with the toes four times, stretch and bend knees alternately (Count 1-4), stretch knees, lie down on the back, relax (Count 5-6) up to starting position (Count 7-8).

7. Hips, back and stretching exercise

(a) Lying on the stomach, hands on the floor in front, head on the hands, raise left leg from the hip (Count 1), down (Count 2), right leg up (Count 3), down (Count 4).

(b) Lying on the stomach, bend the knees, hands grasp each foot, lift the knees from floor and bend backward. "Rockingchair."

8. **Running and jump**

   (a) Join hands in a big circle, face the center. Move to the left. Right foot crossing in front (Count 1) left foot one step to the left (Count 2), right foot crossing behind (Count 3), left foot one step to the side (Count 4), etc. Follow the movement and turn each time to the left and right. Run on tiptoe, stress the footwork, little by little raise your knees higher. Repeat to the right.

   (b) Three steps to the left as (a) (Count 1-3), hop on the right foot, raise left knee (Count 4). Repeat to the right (Count 5-8).

9. **Walking**

   In two ranks, line up along the wall.

10. **For fun and strengthening arms and shoulders**

    Playing the wheelbarrow two by two. One is playing the wheelbarrow, the other moves it. Catch the upper leg. Move forward on the arms. Raise the arm from the shoulder.

11. **Balance exercise**

    (a) Standing with the left leg extended to the left, near the floor. Touch the floor with the toes and "throw" the leg up, higher and higher. Waltz rhythm. Repeat with right leg.

    (b) The same as (a) rising on tiptoe every time the leg is "thrown" up.

12. **Back, side exercise**

    (a) Sitting with legs extended wide apart, hands relaxed on the back. Swing left arm sideways up while bending over the right leg touch the toe, right ear on the right knee (Count 1), stretch farther forward two times (Count 2-3) on count 3 push,  swing left arm up while stretching the back, left arm sideways down to starting position. (Count 4.) Repeat with the right arm, bend to the left (Count 5-8).

    (b) Long sitting, legs together, arms extended forward on the floor, small stretchings further forward.

13. Side exercise

(a) Standing with the feet apart. Move the weight on left foot, bend relaxed to the left side, arms hanging relaxed down (Count 1). Two relaxed bendings deeper down, relaxed knee (Count 2-3), stretch from the waistline to starting position (Count 4). Repeat to the right side.

(b) Standing position as (a), arms extended to the side, shoulder high. Move the weight on left foot, bend to the left, left arm falling relaxed down, right arm raising up, hanging relaxed over the head (Count 1). Two deeper bendings as (a) (Count 2-3), stretch from the waist line to starting position (Count 4). Directly to the right side (Count 5-8).

14. Run

In one line to the stallbar.

15. Back, chest and shoulder exercises

Place your wrists on the bar a little below shoulder height, lean forward from the hips, straight legs, feet a little apart, relaxed neck. Stretch the pectoral by smooth movements downward. No staccato.

16. Back exercise

Lying on the back, head towards the stallbar, arms extended backwards on the floor, catch the lowest bar. Tighten the upper part of the back muscles, raise chest, head hanging relaxed backwards (Count 1-2), to starting position, relax (Count 3-4). The exercise might be done without stall-  bars, the arms only relaxed along the sides.

17. Abdominal and hip benders

Hanging from the highest bar, back against the stallbar, raise left knee (Count 1), down (Count 2), right knee (Count 3), down (Count 4).

18. Running and jump

Run in one line round the floor. Chalk up lines at right angles to the wall approximately one yard apart. Make leaping steps over the lines, try to stretch your knees while the legs are wide apart (one forward, one backward). Leap as high as possible. Free form.

APPARATUS WORK

1st and 2nd week

Tumbling

Headstand with legs hanging down, stretched knees, first step to learning the headspring. See "Tumbling": headspring.

Balance beam

Start the backward roll, low beam, two spotters one on each side. The performer lying on the back on the beam with both hands behind the head, gripping beam (elbows up). Head hanging down on the side of the beam. Move stretched legs slowly up, then faster down to the beam behind the head, get one knee down on the beam, the other stretched leg backwards. (Knee Scale.)

Vaulting box

Practice direct forward roll on the box. Good take-off, hips high start roll immediately after touching the box, tuck head and land on neck and shoulders.

Ropes

Practice climbing the rope.

3rd and 4th week

Tumbling

Free training. The girls practice what they need the most.

Balance beam

Repeat everything.

Vaulting box

Repeat.

Buck

Repeat.

PROGRAM VI

1. Walking, running

2. Foot exercise

(a) Standing position, heels together, toes apart, 90° angle. Move right foot forward, right heel touching the left big toe. Raise the heel of the front foot. Roll down on the heel of the front foot while raising to tiptoe on back foot, etc. Start slowly, then little by little increase the speed. Repeat with the other foot in front.

(b) Same as (a), moving to the side in short steps. Keep the right angle, do not turn the body. Move to the left when the left foot is in front, to the right when the right foot is in front.

3. Arm exercise

(a) Standing position, both arms a little to the right. Relaxed arm swing from one side to the other (low) while relaxing the knees, central back bobbing up and down.[8]

(b) Arm swing as (a), to the left and to the right (Count 1-2), arm swing to the left, up all the way around in a big circle, stretch up, look at the hands (Count 3). Swing the arms to the left (Count 4). Repeat starting the swing to the right.

4. Leg exercise

(a) Standing position, arms extended at 45° angle to body. Raise on tiptoe, bend the knees (half down) with stretched hips, (push the hips a little forward) (Count 1), stretch to start position (Count 2).

(b) Squat position, arms extended at 45° angle to body, stretch the knees halfway up, (push the hips forward) (Count 1-2), down to start position (Count 3-4).

5. Hop

(a) Hop on one foot raising the other knee, (stretch the ankle). Two hops on each foot, moving forwards, even rhythm. (Count 1-2, 3-4.)

[8]Relax as arms swing downward — stretch as they swing upward — JN.

(b) Same hop as (a), moving backwards, the center of gravity a little backwards.

6. Back exercise

(a) Sitting on your heels, arms along the sides. Bend forward, (round upper back, relaxed neck). Swing the arms sideways up, relaxed over head *and* stretch the back. Swing arms forward up (Count 1). Drop the arms sideways down (Count 2).

(b) Sit on your heels, arms extended upwards, bend upper back backwards, small bounces further backwards, smoothly. Shake the arms when finished.

7. Side exercise

Standing on your knees, arms extended forward. Push left hip to the side and sit down on the left (Count 1-2), raise to starting position (Count 3-4), sit down on the right (Count 5-6), to starting position (Count 7-8).

8. Back — side exercise

Long sitting position. Lean forward from the hips, arms extended forward on the floor (Count 1). Stretch farther forwards twice (Count 2-3), turn to the left, swinging left arm to the side and backwards, right hand on (distal part of) left ankle, look at the left hand (Count 4). Stretch further backwards twice, (Count 5-6). Repeat, turn to the right, (Count 1-3, 4-6).

9. Jump

First step to learning the turn jump. Stand on your left foot, right foot extended forward, stretched ankle, toe touching the floor. Jump on the spot turning 90 degrees left. (Stress the abrupt turning of the hips) (Count 1-2). Keep the toe on floor, look forward all the time. Repeat standing on your right foot, etc.

10. Balance exercise

(a) Three gliding steps forward, long-short-long, left, right, left, rise on tiptoe, right leg a little backward, stretch the upper back (Count 1-4). Repeat starting with right foot (Count 1-4), etc.

(b) As (a) with running steps and hop on (Count 4).

11. Back exercise

Standing feet together, legs straight, leaning forward from the hips, arms extended far forward, with hands close to the floor. Touch the floor twice, stretching farther forward, (Count 1-2), swing your arms backwards, relaxing arms, neck, back, and knees, (Count 3), dip your knees while swinging the arms forwards, and rolling the back out[9] forward to starting position (Count 4).

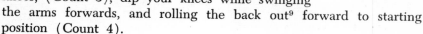

12. Side exercise

Standing with feet together, arms extended upwards, look at the hands. Bend to the left, relax the knees, (Count 1), two deeper relaxed bendings (Count 2-3), stretch from waistline to starting position (Count 4). Repeat to the right side (Count 1-4).

13. For back and feet, and for fun

Standing in four lines, good distance between the lines and between each girl. Two girls make one team, one from each line. We call the lines A, B, C, and D. A and B are partners and C and D. The A's and C's turn 90 degrees, and get down on hands and knees. The B's and the D's sit on floor with crossed legs, hands on their knees. When the teacher says: Ready, go! — the B's and D's run to their partners and creep under. The A's and C's stretch their legs supporting weight on toes and hands (build a "bridge"). The B or D girl back in starting position first has won the game. Repeat several times, then change to letting the A's and C's creep under, etc. Note: The girls are never allowed to "Crawl" on the knees, but must move on hands and feet.

14. Running-steps

Three running-steps forward, left, right, left, hop on left foot, raise right knee (high jump with stretched ankle) (Count 1-4). Repeat starting with the right foot, (Count 1-4), etc.

15. Tumbling

Practice the handstand in couples against the wall. The "swinging" leg touches the wall, the other hanging relaxed. (Repeat.)

---

[9]"Rolling the back": concentration on straightening spine from lower to upper back.

APPARATUS WORK

1st and 2nd week

Bar

Chest high. Take off, jump on the bar, turn hands, legs stretched backward, arch the back. Forward hip circle, rounded back, keep legs stretched sliding round the bar, bend knees in the last moment. Repeat.

Tumbling

(a) Headstand, forward roll (See "Tumbling": headstand).
(b) Second step of headspring (See "Tumbling": headspring).

Vaulting box

Lengthwise. Take off, jump on the box (hips high) land in squat position, jump over with legs bent between the arms. Push away with the arms, look up. Two spotters.

Ropes

Climbing and vaults. Repeat.

3rd and 4th week

Balance beam

Jump up on one foot to squat position at the end of the beam. Place hands so far forward that there is room for the foot behind. The other leg hanging relaxed down. Stretch to standing, walk, run or move forwards in short jumps. Sit down in squat position and rise again. Jump down.

Tumbling

Headspring, third step, (See "Tumbling": headspring).

Vaulting box-lengthwise

As 1st and 2nd week, try to place the hands far forward, later at the far end of the box. Then jump all the way over. Two spotters.

Buck

Crosswise. Straddle vault.

PROGRAM VII

1. Walking, running

In waltz rhythm 1-2-3 (long-short-short). First step rolling down on full foot, relaxing the knee, 2 steps on tiptoe.

2. Arm exercise

Standing position. Left arm swing forward up, all the way round in a big circle, relaxing and stretching back and knees, 2 times, (Count 1-2), swing left arm relaxed forward and backward, relax back and knees (Count 3-4). Use the left arm several times, repeat with right arm.

3. Leg exercise

(a) Standing position. Move left foot a little forward, deep knee bending, on tiptoe, 2 further bendings (Count 1-3), stretch up to a standing position, left foot in front of right (Count 4-6). Repeat, moving the right foot forward.

(b) As (a) with relaxed neck and back.

4. Back exercise

(a) Leading up to the succeeding back exercise. Standing position, arms extended forward shoulder distance apart. Tighten the abdominal muscles, round the central part of the back, relax the knees (Count 1-2) to starting position (Count 3-4).

(b) Standing position. Upper body bent forward (rounded upper back, relaxed neck) arms swinging sideways up relaxed, bent over head, relax knees, *and* stretching the back and knees, swing the arms forward up (Count 1). Drop the arms relaxed to the sides and down (Count 2). The exercise goes on continuously without stopping in any position. Use the back muscles when stretching. (See Program VI, Exercise 6.)

(c) As (b) rising on tiptoe.

(d) Standing position, bending upper back backwards (Count 1-2) stretching to starting position (Count 3-4). Bend relaxed forward, shake arms, shoulders and neck.

Students from University of Oslo Gymnastic Club show different kinds of balance stand

5. Jump

(a) Standing position. Move 3 steps to the left, starting with right foot crossing (Count 1-3), hop on right foot swinging left foot to the side (Count 4). Two hops in place on left foot, swinging right leg to the side (Count 5-6), two hops on right foot swinging the left leg (Count 7-8). Repeat starting with the left foot crossing, etc. (See Program IV, Exercise 7.)

(b) In couples, joining inner hands, good distance between the 2 partners. As (a) moving forward, 45° to the side (Count 1-8, 1-8).

6. Leg exercise

Standing position, move left foot to the side, landing on tiptoe, weight on left foot, bent knee, left arm extended shoulder high to the side, turn the head to the left (Count 1), push the weight to the right foot, raise left leg a little with stretched knee (Count 2), left foot crossing in front, one step to the right, lower left arm (Count 3). Repeat to the right (Counts 4-6). (See Program I, Exercise 8.)

7. Side exercise

Standing on the right knee, left leg extended to the side, foot on floor with toes pointing forward, right arm extended shoulder high to the side. Drop the arm relaxed down crossing in front (Count 1). Arm swing sideways up (Count 2), side bending to the left, right arm hanging relaxed over the head (Count 3), one deeper bending and stretching with the arm swinging up (Count 4), etc. Repeat on the left knee bending to the right side. Sit down to the right, lie down on the back, arms relaxed along the sides.

8. Abdominal exercise

Lying on the back, rise to sitting position with bent knees, feet off floor, arms extended forward, the head on the knees (Count 1-3), down to starting position (Count 4-6). When finished rise on the knees, bend the toes, move the weight backward and get up to standing position.

9. Hop

Hop twice on the right foot while swinging left leg forward from the hip (Count 1-2). Two hops on the right foot while left leg swings backwards (Count 3-4), four hops on the left foot, right leg swinging forward and backwards (Count 5-8), etc.

10. Side exercise

Standing position, turn from one side to the other, swinging the arms relaxed from side to side around the body, relaxed knees (Count 1-2), feet together in place. (Waltz rhythm.)

11. Balance exercise

In couples, standing position joining inner hands. Raise left leg backward from the hip moving the upper part of the body forward to balance stand (Count 1-4), return to standing position, do not drop the leg (Count 5-8). Keep the back arched. (See Program III, Exercise 11.)

12. Handstand exercise

Starting position for handstand, see "Tumbling": handstand. Swing back leg up, the other leg hanging down, (Count: up — and down).

13. Back — abdominal exercise

In couples, facing each other, one sitting with legs crossed, the other long sitting, feet against the legs of the partner. Join hands. The one bends backwards with arched back, the head touching the floor, the second bending forward (Count 1-4), to starting position (Count 5-8). Several times. Repeat changing leg position.

14. Jump

In two lines around the gym floor. Hop one step forward on the left foot (Count 1), step forward right (Count 2), one hopping step on the right foot while raising left knee (Count 3). Repeat several times.

15. Cartwheel

In two lines along the wall back to the wall standing in zig zag. First step learning the cartwheel. See "Tumbling": cartwheel.

APPARATUS WORK I

Balance beam

(a) Practice the jump up on the end of the beam.

(b) Move forward, swing left leg forward up (Count 1), dip and stretch standing knee (Count 2). Two steps on tiptoe left and right (Count 3-4) 3 steps forward starting left, raise right leg backward (Count 5-8). Repeat with the right leg swinging forward.

Tumbling

(a) Headstand forward roll, forward roll, 2 hare-jumps, forward, finish with a high jump.

(b) Forward roll to sitting position on one foot, the other leg extended forward.

(c) Practice backwards roll.

Vaulting box

The box 45 degree angle to the running direction. Start with outside foot, 3 running steps, take off on starting foot, place inside hand on the nearest end of the box, swing inside leg high up, then the take off leg, closed feet over the box. The other hand is placed on the box behind the girl's back and helps to push her over. Land on the floor on the opposite side. Rhythm: *1-2-3* jump.

APPARATUS WORK II

Balance beam

(a) Practice sitting down on the beam and rising to standing position.
(b) Lying on the back, backwards roll.

Tumbling

Headspring. 4th step, (See "Tumbling": headspring).

Vaulting box

As I.

Buck

Straddle jump, make the buck higher.

PROGRAM VIII

1. **Walking, running**

   Hop forward, one hop on each foot, jump sideways, free form.

2. **Arm and leg exercise**

   Move forward. Left foot on tiptoe, raise right knee, swing the arms forward, up sideways down *1*-2-3 in a big circle. Repeat on the right foot (Mazurka rhythm).

3. **Back exercise**

   Standing position. Swing arms forward (as knees and back relax and stretch (Count 1), then raise left arm, bend upper back backward (Count 2), deeper bending then stretch the back (Count 3), arms fall forward and down, as upper back and neck bend relaxed forward (Count 4).

4. **Side exercise**

   Standing position. Swing arms forward relaxing and stretching knees and central back (Count 1), twist to the left, swing arms down, backwards on the left side (Count 2), turn forward swinging arms down forward (Count 3), drop arms down a little backwards (Count 4). All the time, relax and stretch the knees and the back. In the turned position, "hang" backwards, push front hip forward. Repeat to the right.

5. **Jump**

   (a) Reel. Raise left knee, put left foot behind the right, hop on left foot while raising right knee (Count 1), put right foot behind the left, hop on the right while raising left knee (Count 2), etc. Start slowly, then speed up little by little.

   (b) Four hops on one foot while turning 360° to the left and right. When turning to the left, hop on right foot with left leg extended to the side, toes pointing to the floor (Count 1-4), change foot and turn to the right hopping on the left foot (Count 5-8).

   (c) Put (a) and (b) together. Four reel steps (Count 1-4), turn 360° (Count 5-8), another four reel steps, turn the other way around (Count 1-8).

6. Side exercise

Standing with the feet apart. Bend to the left, move the weight on to left foot, hang relaxed to the side, relax the arms, neck and left knee (Count 1-2), stretch from the waistline to standing position (Count 3-4). Repeat to the right (Count 5-8).

7. Abdominal exercise

Lying on the back, arms relaxed along the sides. Raise stretched legs (Count 1-4), bend the knees (Count 5-6), slide the legs relaxed to starting position (Count 7-8). Repeat.

8. Hip exercise

Sit with bent knees, knees apart, arms between the legs, hands grasping the heels. Stretch the legs forward up, legs wide apart (Count 1-2), to starting position (Count 3-4). Keep your balance and stretch the back.

9. Back — shoulder exercise

Longsitting with feet extended directly forward, arms extended upward. Bend far forward from the hips, look forward, one hand on each side of the legs (Count 1), three stretchings farther forward (Count 2-4), stretch to starting position (Count 5), three times moving the arms farther backwards from shoulders (Count 6-8).

10. Balance exercise

(a) Standing with the arms extended about 45° to the sides. Swing left leg backwards out in a circle two times (waltz rhythm, Count 1-2), three steps forward on tiptoe (left, right, left, Count 3-4). Repeat, beginning on the right. Swing from the hip with long relaxed leg.

(b) As (a) moving backwards.

(c) As (a) rising on tiptoe when swinging the leg: "*up* and *up.*"

11. Back exercise

Sitting on the heels, bend forward, rounded back head tucked in, arms relaxed on floor along the legs. Stretch upper back forward "roll out," look up (Count 1-4), relax the back, to starting position (Count 5-8).

12. Thigh exercise

Sitting on the heels, arms extended forward, lean a little backwards. Stretch the hips, keep the angle (shanks — thighs) as acute as possible (Count 1-2), to starting position (Count 3-4).

13. **Back — feet exercise**

    Standing on knees and hands, ankles extended. Stretch the knees, hips high, stretched ankles, rise on toenails (Count 1-2), return to starting position (Count 3-4).

14. **Arms and shoulder exercise**

    (a) Squat position, arms extended forward, hare-jumps on the spot, hips high, land on tiptoe (Count 1-2) *Up* and down repetition.

    (b) Same as (a) moving forwards and backwards.

15. **Jumps**

    Moving forward. Mazurka with knee raising (see Program VII, Exercise 14). Three times (Count *1*-2-3, *4*-5-6, 7-8-9), three running steps on tiptoe (Count 10-12). Repeat on the other foot.

APPARATUS WORK

Tumbling

Roll a mat or use the small upper part of the vaulting box. Headspring, next step with two or three spotters, the two sitting on each end of the box, the third holding the legs of the performer, helping her to lean over to find the right angle and helping with the snap.

Vaulting box (lengthwise)

Practice more jumping in squat position, hands should be on the farthest end (the neck) of the box. Get the hips high and little by little place the hands further forward on the box. Lastly, jump all the way over. Push with hands and look up in the last part of the jump. Use two spotters.

Balance beam

Jump up on the end of the beam, move forward in different jumps or steps, try to combine some of the known floor exercises with forward, backward roll in a little series.

Tumbling

(a) Combine two or three different exercises in a little series.
(b) Practice cartwheel.

Buck (crosswise)

Straddle vault and continue practicing as the height of the buck is elevated.

PROGRAM IX

1. Walking, running

Walk to squads, good distance between each person. Walk on the spot, stress the footwork, move forwards, backwards.

2. Arm, back exercise

Standing position. Armswing sideways up, bend upper back forward, relax knees (Count 1) (See program VII, Exercise 4b). One relaxed dipping and stretching, arms extended upwards (Count 2). Swing the arms sideways, down, and forward (Count 3). Swing arms down, sideways up to shoulder height (Count 4). On Count 3 and 4 relax and stretch knees and central back.

3. Back exercise

(a) Standing with the feet a little apart, bend forward from the hips, move both arms relaxed to the right side (Count 1). Swing the arms and turn the upper part of the body relaxed from side to side, look at the hands (Count 2) dipping up and down from the hips all the time. Waltz rhythm.

(b) Same as (a), swinging to the left (Count 1), to the right (Count 2), to the left, stretch and jump high straight up (Count 3). Repeat starting the swing to the right (Count 4-6).

4. Jump, leg exercise (Second step to "turn jump.")

(a) Standing position. Swing left leg forward (high), backwards, forward, raise on the tiptoe on the right (Count 1-3). Turn from the hips 180° to the right (Count 4). Go on with left leg swinging, turning to the right. Repeat with the right leg swinging, turn to the left.

(b) Same as (a). Turn with a high jump straight up on Count 4.

5. Leg exercise

Standing position. Move left foot a long step to the left, land on tiptoe, bend your left knee (Count 1), bend the knee further (Count 2-3), push with left foot stretch the knee and ankle, moving the weight on to right foot (Count 4) to starting position (Count 5-6). Repeat to the right side.

6. Back exercise

(a) Lying on the stomach, arms along the sides. Bend backwards, move only the upper back (Count 1-2), to starting position and relax (Count 3-4).

(b) As (a) with arms extended forward.

7. Abdominal exercise

(a) (Upper part) Lying on the back, arms along the sides. Sit halfway up with rounded back, the head starts the movement, chin to chest (Count 1-3). Roll piece by piece down to starting position, relax  (Count 4-6). Start with the lower part of the back, then the upper part and finally the head.

(b) (Lower part) *Hipbenders*. Lying on the back, left knee bent, right leg extended upwards, "Cycling," bend and stretch knees and ankles, lower your legs close to the floor and up, raise them again — while cycling all the time (Count 1-2) (Repetition).

8. Side exercise

Standing on left knee, right knee extended to the side, bend to the left, move right arm sideways up and over the head (Count 1-4), stretch to starting position (Count 5-8). Several times to the left, then repeat to the right standing on right knee.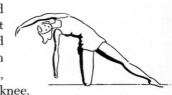

9. Jump

(a) Three running steps, *l,r,l*, hop straight up on left foot, raise the right leg backwards, arch the back (Count 1-4). Repeat right, left, right, etc. (Count 5-8). (See Program VI, Exercise 10b.)

(b) Three running steps, hop, raise one knee (Count 1-4), repeat with the other foot (Count 5-8). (See Program VI, Exercise 14.)

(c) Do (a) + (b). (a) twice (Count 1-4, 5-8), and (b) twice (Count 1-4, 5-8).

10. Balance exercise

(a) Standing position, arms extended forward, shoulder high, left leg extended backwards, stretched knee, toe pointing against the floor. Raise left leg from the hip (Count 1-2), to starting position (Count 3-4). Repeat.

(b) Starting position as in (a). Start as (a) (Count 1-2), move the leg (higher) to balance stand (Count 3-4), raise to starting position (Count 5-8). Repeat with right leg extended backwards.

11. Back, abdominal exercise

In couples, longsitting, inner hands joined, arms hanging down. Bend f o r w a r d from the hips, arms stretched relaxed forward on the floor (Count 1). Stretching further forward (Count 2-3), stretch to starting position, (Count 4). Lean backwards, stretched back, raise the arms forward up, (Count 5-6). Stretch to starting position. Move the arms forward down. (Count 7-8).

12. For fun — "Grinding Pepper"

In couples, facing each other, join crossed hands, lean backwards, arms stretched, closed feet. Move to the left with small steps, increase the speed. Repeat to the right.

13. (Repetition.) Skip forward, small jumps,

Watch the footwork.

APPARATUS WORK

Balance beam

(a) Practice the small series started in Program VIII.

(b) For the girls who can do: the handstand correctly by the wall, and the cartwheel on the floor. Then start with the Low Beam. Start the cartwheel dismounting from the end of the beam. One spotter, behind the performer. Performer goes into movement and keeps legs joined when passing handstand, landing on both feet on the mat at the end of the beam.

Tumbling

(a) Practice the small series started in Program VIII.

(b) Practice cartwheel to both sides.

(c) Practice the headstand, snap to handstand with one spotter. (See *Tumbling* headspring third step.)

Vaulting box

(a) Take off, forward roll. Land on shoulders, get the hips high. Little by little move the springboard farther from the box.

(b) Practice jumping over the box, hands on the farthest end (See Program VIII).

Buck (Crosswise) Right and Left Flank Vaults

Take off, jump over the buck with both legs swinging to the same side (left and right).

Handstand

Practice handstand by the wall and on the floor. Work in couples.

PROGRAM X

1. Walking, running

4 steps on the heels, 1-4, 4 steps high up on tiptoe 5-8.

2. Arm exercise

(a) Standing position. Swing left arm forward up and round in a big circle, relax and stretch back and knees, 2 times 1-2, relaxed swing forward, backward 3-4; continue several times with left arm, repeat with the right.

(b) The same as *a* using both arms.

3. Leg exercise

Squat position, keep the back straight and the arms a little forward. Raise a bit stretching the hips and leaning backwards 1-2, to starting position 3-4.

4. Back exercise

(a) Standing with the arms extended upwards. Drop the arms sideways down, crossing your wrists in front of the body, bend upper back forward, rounded back, relax neck and knees 1, dipping and stretching your knees, back and neck to starting position, arms swinging sideways up 2.

(b) Starting position as *a*. Bend upper back backwards, small stretchings farther backwards *1* and *2* and. . .

(c) *a* + *b* put together, a 1-2, b 3-4. (Bend backwards and stretch.)

5. Back exercise

Standing, feet apart. Bend relaxed forward down to the left, touching the floor three times outside left heel, relaxed bounces 1-3, stretch to starting position on 4. Repeat to the right 5-8.

6. Jump

Standing position. (Moving sideways.) 1 hopping step to the left on left foot (1), right foot one step to the left, crossing in front (2), hop on right foot, left leg swinging to the side (3). Continue. Repeat to the right. Mazurka rhythm.

7. Side exercise

Standing with the arms extended upwards. Bend
to the left relaxing knees (1), one relaxed bounce
farther to the side (2), drop left arm sideways
down, crossing in front of the body bouncing again
(3), dipping knees, stretch to starting position,
left arm swinging sideways up (4). Repeat to the
right.

8. Abdominal exercise

(a) Standing on knees, arms extended forward. Bend backwards from the knees, raise
left arm 1-3, stretch to starting position 4-6.
Repeat raising right arm.

(b) Jump to squat position, arms extended forward. Hare-jumps on
the spot, hips high.

Students from University of Oslo Gymnastics Club showing Abdominal Exercise

9. Balance exercise

In couples, join inner hands. Raise outside
knee, catch the heel on the inside 1-2,
stretch the knee forward up, a little to the
side 3-4, bend the knee, to starting position
5-6, about, face 7-8. Repeat with the other
leg, 1-8, etc.

10. **Hops**

    In couples, join inner hands, feet in 90° angle, left heel to the right big toe. (See Program VI, Exercise 2b.) Move sideways left foot short step to the left (1), right foot behind (2), repeat 3-4, 5-6. 2 small hops on left foot, right leg swinging to the side (low). Repeat to the right, etc. Use the ankles rolling down on the heel and up on tiptoe.

11. **Back, side exercise**

    In couples, facing each other, join both hands. "Pancaketurn" 360° turn in place, under the arms, taking 4 small steps high up on tiptoe and swinging the arms sideways up and around in a big circle 1-4, repeat the opposite way 5-8, etc.

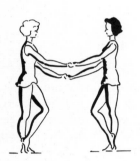 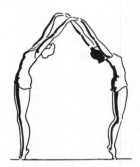

12. **Side exercise**

    In couples, facing each other, join crossed hands, stretched arms. Drop left arm down and out to shoulder-height, turn to the left and hang backwards, looking at the back hand 1, to starting position, left arm swinging down and forward 2. Repeat to the right, etc., 3-4.

13. **Abdominal exercise**

    Lying on the back, arms relaxed along the sides. Raise both knees, feet off floor 1, stretch your legs forward, close to the floor 2, bend your knees 3, stretch straight up 4, lower the legs to starting position, relax 5-8.

14. **Leap**

    3 running steps, "scissor leaps" 1-4. Left foot starts forward then right, left and take off 1-3, swing right leg forward up from the hip — left leg swinging up and passing right leg 4. Land on right foot and continue, r.l.r., etc.

Apparatus Work

Balance beam

(a) Repeat the known exercises.

(b) Train to sit down on the beam and rise on one foot, to one leg, squat and return: Standing position, raise one leg, bend standing knee, put your hands on the beam, behind the hips, sit down keeping your legs stretched about 45-60° above the beam. Bending one knee, place the foot on the beam and swing the other leg down, and backward rising to standing position on one foot.

Tumbling

(a) Continue the headspring training.

(b) Start the backward roll with extension to handstand.

Buck

(Crosswise) (a) Straddle vault.
(b) Jump over the buck in squat position.

Vaulting box

(Oblique) 3 running steps: l.r.l., take off on 3, touch the box with right hand, swing right leg forward up, then left leg, keep both legs close together when passing the box, body and legs in acute angle, push with left and, landing on both feet. Count: *1*-2-3-jump: Practice to the opposite side.

PROGRAM XI

1. Walking, running

Running in waltz rhythm 1-2-3. Walking to 4 lines.

2. Arm exercise

Standing position, arms swing forward (1), armswing down, backward, sideways up in a big circle, twice (2-3) arms fall forward, down a little backward (4); all the time relax and stretch knees and back. Full stretch when the arms swing up.

3. Leg exercise

Squat position, fingertips on the floor at sides. (First step leading up to "long fall forward.") Shift weight on the right foot with the hips just over right heel, with left leg extended backward. Raise upper trunk, arms extended to the sides, shoulder-high. Small dippings in the front knee. Repeat with right leg extended backward (short duration).

4. Back exercise

Standing position. Arms swing forward up, (1), lower the arms a little sideways, bend upper back backwards (2). Bend farther back smoothly then stretch (3), bend forward with rounded upper back, the arms falling forward, down and a little backward, relax knees (4) with knees dipping, arms swing forward up, stretched knees and back, repeat the exercise. (See Program VII, Exercise 4b.)

5. Jump

Standing position, arms extended to the sides shoulder-high. 2 hops on right foot, left leg swinging forwards from the hip 1-2, another 2 hops on right foot, left leg swinging backward 3-4. Repeat the hops on left foot, right leg swinging. (Repetition.)

6. Side exercise

(a) Basic exercise. Standing position relax central back and knees 1-2, stretch from the center 3-4.

(b) Standing position, left arm extended to the side, shoulder-high. Drop the left arm relaxed crossing in front, relax back and knees (See a) 1. Swing left arm sideways up, bend and stretch knees and back (stretch the whole body, press the feet against the floor) 2. Deep bending to the right, relaxed knees, left arm hanging relaxed over the head 3, deeper bending, dipping the knees and stretching from the waistline, swinging left arm up to position "1" 4. Continue several times, then repeat with right arm, bending to the left.

7. Back exercise

Longsitting, arms crossed, bend forward raise the arms a little, chest against the knees, look forward (1), stretch to starting position 2, repeat 3-4, bend forward, arms stretched forward 5, 2 bounces farther forward, one hand on either side of the legs, relaxed arms (6-7), stretch the back to starting position (8) and start again 1, etc.

8. Abdominal exercise

(a) Lying on the back, bend and stretch the knees, roll up on the neck (1-2), pause (3), bend and stretch the knees, roll down to starting position (4-5), relax (6). Continue. Mazurka rhythm. Last time stop in the neck-standing position.

(b) Move left leg backwards down to the floor behind the head and raise (1-2), repeat with right leg (3-4). Move both legs backwards down, toes on the floor behind the head, swing the legs fast forward bending the knees, and get up to standing position with a high jump.

9. Balance exercise

In couples, join inner hands. (a) Standing with left leg extended backwards knee and ankle stretched, toes pointing against the floor. Raise left leg backward from the hip, keep the body straight up (1-2), to starting position (3-4). Continue several times. Repeat with right leg. (Repetition.) (b) Standing, raise left leg backwards, up from the hip to balance stand, arched back (1-4), raise to starting position, keep the leg high and keep the back muscles tightened (5-8). Repeat with right leg. Finally stop for control in balance — front scale — supporting leg should be straight.

10. Handstand

Hands on the floor to starting position. (See Tumbling, handstand.) Swing up to handstand, one leg extended, the other hanging. Count, or use music (slowly) *up!* — and down! etc.

11. Jump

(a) Repeat Exercise 11, Program IV.

(b) Moving forward, 2 hops on right foot, bend left knee as *a* 1-2, 2 hops on left foot, bending right knee 3-4 .

12. Hip exercise

Standing position, left foot behind the right and turned a little to the left, left arm extended to the side. Swing left leg to the side, try to touch the left hand without turning the hips 1, to starting position, relaxing right knee 2. Repeat swinging right leg.

13. Side, back exercise

Standing position, feet apart, arms extended upwards. Bend to the left (1-4), turn to the left, bend relaxed forward, arms hanging (5), 3 bounces farther forward against the floor (6-8). Turn to side-bending and raise to starting position (1-2), bend to the right side (3-4), turn and bend relaxed forward (5). 3 bounces farther forward (6-8). The exercise goes directly from side to side.

14. Leaping steps

Push with the right and leap forward on left foot (long and high leap left leg extended forward, right leg extended backwards) (1). 2 running steps r.l. (2-3), repeat with right leg extended forward in a long and high leap, etc. (4-6). Mazurka rhythm.

Apparatus Work

Bar

"Walking" sideways by the arms, swinging the body from side to side (from the shoulder).

Tumbling

(a) Handstand, forward roll (work in couples).
(b) Handstand, forward roll, directly to squat position, another forward roll, finish with a high jump, swinging the arms forward up.

Vaulting box

(Crosswise) Repeat Flank Vaults. Jump over, swinging both legs to the same side without turning. Practice to both sides.

Balance beam

Free work. Try to combine the known exercises (to a short routine).

Tumbling 11

Mats and the upper part of the vaulting box. Practice the headspring. The student works on her personal level. Step 1,2,3 or 4.

Buck

(High) Straddle vault. Stress perfect landing.

PROGRAM XII

1. **Walking, running**

    Form a big circle. Running on the spot, roll on the feet, raise the knees slightly higher and jump.

2. **Stretching exercise**

    Standing, arms extended upward, reach upward left arm and side, then the right side. Count: "Stretch — and stretch," etc. Bend forward, relax, neck, back and knees, move slightly up and down in the knees, roll up the back.

3. **Back exercise**

    Lie down on the stomach, relaxed legs (joined toes, heels apart) one hand under each shoulder, fingers pointing forward. The head starts the bending backward, stretch the arms gradually, keep the hips on the floor (1-4), to starting position, piece by piece, head at last, relax (5-8). Repetition. (See Program II, Exercise 12.)

4. **Hip exercise**

    Lying on the stomach, arms crossed, head on arms. Swing left leg backwards from hips (high) (1), lower the leg to the floor on right side (cross over, approximately 90°) (2). Raise up to position "1" (3), to starting position (4). Repeat with the right leg (5-8).

5. **Back exercise**

    (a) Sitting on the heels, tuck position, arms relaxed along the legs. Roll the upper back forward to approximately 45°, look at the ceiling, arched back (1-3), roll down to starting position, relax (4-6).

    (b) Sitting on the heels, tuck position, arms on the floor, fingers pointing forwards. Roll the back forwards, up, lean backwards raising the arms as well, arch the back (1-3), roll down to starting position, relax (4-6).

6. **Jump**

    (a) (Moving forward) 2 hops on right foot, bend left knee turned approximately 45° to the left, foot behind right knee (1-2), repeat bending right knee (3-4). (See Program 11, Exercise 2b.) 4 hops in the same way: r.l.r.l. (5-8), etc.

(b) Jump moving backward. 2 hops on right foot, left knee raised slightly forward (1-2), repeat the hop on left foot, raising right knee (3-4), repeat (5-6), (7-8).

(c) *a + b* together, *a* (1-8), *b* (1-8).

7. Arms, side exercise

(a) Standing position, left arm extended to the side, shoulder high. Drop the arm relaxed across in front, relax back and knees (1), dip knees, swing the arm and stretch knees and back to starting position (2). Repeat with the right.

(b) Standing position, left arm extended to the side, bend slightly to the left. Slightly bend and stretch the arm farther to the side, relax and stretch central back and knees. The movement is like a wave through the whole body (sideways). Keep the whole foot on the floor and the weight on both feet. Practice a while with left arm, repeat with the right.

8. Leg exercise

In couples, join inner hands. Swing left leg forward, backward, forward (1-3), and backward, rising on tiptoe (4). Bend right knee, left leg extended backward, ankle on the floor (5). 2 dippings in the front knee, and stretching to starting position (6-8). Repeat with right leg swinging (1-8).

9. Jump

Standing on the right foot, left leg extended (low) to the side. Move sideways to the left jumping on the right foot while clapping the feet together (in the air) on each jump. Lean a little to the right. Repeat to the right side, jumping on left foot.

10. Abdominal exercise

Standing on the right knee, left knee bent, foot on floor in front, arms extended forward. Bend backward from the hips, raise left arm (1-4), stretch and lower the arm, to starting position (5-8). 3-4 times on right foot. Repeat standing on left knee, moving right arm.

11. Side exercise

Standing on both knees, arms extended forward. Move the hips to the left, sit down slowly on the left side of the legs (1-2), raise to starting position (3-4), repeat to the right side (5-6), (7-8). Move slowly from side to side continuously. Repetition. (See Program VI, Exercise 7.)

12. Stretching exercise

Sitting in hurdle position. Bend slightly forward between the legs, arms relaxed forward on the floor. Small, smooth stretchings farther forward (short duration). Repeat with the other leg bent.

13. Running, side exercise

(a) Repeat running in waltz rhythm. (See Program VII, Exercise 1.)

(b) Standing position, arms extended to the sides, alternately relaxed bending and stretching the arms, sidebending and sidewave (1-3), (4-6). (See this program, Exercise 7b.)

(c) Put *a* and *b* together, start with left foot while bending to the left, etc.

14. Handstands

Starting position, for handstands by the wall, the "wrong" leg back. Swing up to handstand, one leg hanging. Up! — and down!

Apparatus Work

Balance beam

(low) (a) Backward roll, up on one knee, hands on the beam, the other leg extended up backwards, back arched, (knee scale), head up. Drop the back leg, raise the back, arms extended forward, move the "hanging" leg forward, place the foot on the beam, rise to standing position.

(b) (higher beam) Practice running steps, jump up on the end of the beam, land on one foot, try to rise to standing position as fast as possible. Practice different jumps, moving forward, pirouettes, etc.

Vaulting box (lengthwise)

Jump over the box placing hands on the farthest end of it. Keep body at an angle of 30° — 45° with the box, hips and knees stretched. This is marked for a moment only. Then bend knees and hips, push with the hands, jump through, raise head and land on the mat.

Ropes

Climb up the rope as high as each student can manage, go slowly down.

Tumbling

(a) Practice the headspring, each student at her level.

(b) Cartwheel.

Buck

Straddle vault (high buck).

PROGRAM XIII

1. Walking, running

Walking forward, (a) arms swinging relaxed a little higher than usual. Start putting the toes on the floor, then roll down on full foot. Roll up on tiptoe on left foot when right toe takes the floor. Relax and stretch central back and knees (the whole body bobbing up and down), (b) running forward.

2. Arm, side exercise

Standing position, left arm extended to the side, shoulder high. Drop left arm crossing in front of the body, relax back and knees, (1), dipping your knees swing left arm sideways up in a big circle, stretch knees and back (2), left arm continues to the right, down, and out to starting position, lilting movement, flexible knees, bend a little to the left (3). Slightly bend and stretch left arm farther to the side, relax and stretch knees and back (sidewave) (4). Continue several times with left arm. Repeat with the right.

3. Leg exercise

Standing position. Fall forward on left foot (long step), land on tiptoe, front leg bent, back leg stretched, extended backward, ankle on the floor. Bounce front knee twice and rise to starting position, moving back leg forward (Count 1-4). Repeat landing on the right foot.

4. Back exercise

(a) (Basic exercise) Standing position, arms extended forward, round central back, tightening the abdominal muscles, relax the knees (1-2), to starting position (3-4). Repetition. (See Program VII, Exercise 4a.)

(b) As *a*, rolling high up on tiptoe. (See Program VII, Exercise 4a.)

(c) Standing position, left arm extended to the side, palm backwards, rounded arm. Swing the arm forward and backward, "drawing" a horizontal figure 8, flexible knees *1-2-3*. Swinging backward, the arm turns round (palm forward). *4-5-6*. Waltz. Little by little let head and body follow the movement. Tighten the abdominal muscles when arms are swinging forward, push hips forward, bend the upper back and head backward when arms are moving backward (small bodywaves). Repeat with right arm extended to the side.

(d) Same exercise as *c* using both arms.

5. Back exercise

(a) Standing position. Swing the arms forward, dipping knees (1) bend forward stretched knees, touch the floor with the fingertips far in front (2), relax neck, back and knees, swing the arms relaxed backward (3). Dipping your knees stretch back to standing position, swing the arms forward, up sideways down (4) to new (1-4).

(b) Same exercise as *a*, rising to tiptoe on *4*.

(c) Same exercise as *a*, jumping straight up on *4*.

6. Jump

Standing position. Three running steps to the left, right foot starts, crossing in front 1-2, jump on 3, swing left leg to the side, clap your feet together and land on right foot 4, hopping on the spot twice on left foot, swinging right leg to the side 5-6, twice on right, swinging left leg to the side 7-8. Repeat moving to the right, left foot starting 1-8, etc.

7. Side exercise

(a) Standing position, arms extended upwards. Bend to the left, relaxed knees (1), deeper bendings, flexible knees (2), another deep bending, drop left arm crossing in front (3), knee-dipping, swing left arm sideways up, stretch from the waistline to starting position (4). Repeat to the right (5-8), etc.

(b) Same exercise as *a*. When dropping left arm move left foot crossing in front, (weight on the front door). Repeat to the right.

8. Abdominal, side exercise

Sit on the floor, both legs to the left side, left leg stretched right leg bent, right knee on the floor, arms extended forward. Swing both legs forward bent knees, feet off the floor (1), stretch the legs forward up (2), swing the legs to the right side, stretch the right leg (3-4). Move your legs slowly nonstop from side to side. Lie down and relax.

9. Foot exercise

Lying on the back, bent knees, feet on the floor, toes together, heels apart. Raise heels, stretch the ankles 1-2, to starting position, relax 3-4. (Repetition.) Shake one leg at the time (straight up).

10. Abdominal exercise

Lying on the back, roll up on the neck, legs stretched upwards, elbows on the floor, hands on the hips. Bend left knee and start cycling while rolling down on the back, rising to sitting position. Continue the cycling rolling down on the back, etc. Repetition.

11. Back exercise

(a) Standing on your knees, hands on the floor, shoulders, hips and knees in 90° angle. Tighten the abdominal muscles, round the back, head tucked in (1-2), arch the back, raise head and look at the ceiling (3-4).

(b) Standing on your knees as *a*. Move left leg backward up, right arm forward up, arch the back, head up (1-4), lower leg and arm to starting position (5-8). Repeat with the right leg and left arm (1-4, 5-8).

12. Jumping steps.

Mazurka rhythm. (a) Leap forward, land on left foot (1), step forward on right foot (2), 2 hops on right foot, raise left knee, stretched ankle 3, continue several times. Repeat on the right foot, raise right knee (1-3), etc. Repetition.

(b) Three times *a* on left foot (1-3), (4-6), (7-9), three running steps forward (10-12), continue on right foot (1-3, 4-6, 7-9), three running steps forward (10-12), etc. Repetition.

Apparatus Work

Balance beam
Free practice.

Tumbling
(a) Practice the cartwheel, each student at her level.
See "Tumbling," cartwheel.

(b) Head-spring.

Vaulting box

Lengthwise. (a) Practice the jump described in Program XII.

(b) Crosswise. Jump with both legs to one side. R. & L. flank vaults. See program XI.

Buck

Straddle vault on high buck.

Tumbling 11.

(a) Handstands, forward roll. Work in couples.

(b) Make up short routines of forward rolls, backward rolls, jump and turn 180°, headstands, hare-jumps, etc.

PROGRAM XIV

1. **Walking, running**

   Skip (one hop on each foot, moving forward).

2. **Arm and leg exercise**

   (a) Standing, left leg extended backward, close to the floor, left arm extended forward. Relaxed leg swing forward, backward left and right arm swinging forward and backward diagonally. (Left arm swing forward when left leg swings backward, etc.) Repeat with the opposite arm and leg.

   (b) As *a*, roll high up on tiptoe in each swing.

   (c) As *a*, small jumps.

3. **Back exercise**

   (a) Standing position, arms extended to the sides, shoulder high. Swing the arms forward and backward "drawing figure eight." When swinging forward, relax knees and back, when backward stretch and bend the upper back backward.
   (Small bodywave.) Waltz. Repetition (See Program XIII, Exercise 4c).

   (b) Standing, arms extended upward. Bend the upper back backwards, small stretchings further backward, smoothly, Waltz rhythm. Keep weight forward.

   (c) *a + b* as follows: Exercise *a* twice (1-4), on 4 raise the arms outside up. Bend upper back backward (5). 2 stretchings further backward (6-7), (on 7 stretch upwards as well), arms falling forward and down and out to starting position, relaxing and stretching back and knees (8-9).

4. **Back exercise**

   Starting position. Standing, b a c k rounded forward, relaxed neck, arms and knees. Roll out the back, raise arms forward up, stretch knees, 90° angle in the hips, look at the ceiling (1-4),  relax, to starting position (5), pause (6-8). The relaxing ought to be smooth (like the air streaming out of a balloon).

5. **Jump**

   (a) Standing, arms extended a little to the sides. Three running steps backward (on tiptoe, stress the footwork), left foot starts (1-3). On 3, hop on left foot, right leg swinging to the side and backward "drawing" a bow, as high as possible (4). Repeat starting the right foot (5-8), etc.

(b) Repeat: hop moving forward, raise alternate knee, 2 hops on each foot (1-2), (3-4), etc.

(c) Put *a* + *b* together. *b* 4 times (1-2), (3-4), (5-6), (7-8). *a* twice (1-4), (5-8).

6. Side exercise

Standing on right knee, left leg extended to the side, the whole foot on floor, toes and knee in one line, arms extended to the left (right arm bent in front of the body), shoulder high. Swing arms down to the right, right arm continues all the way up (1), bend to the left side, right arm hanging long and relaxed over the head, left arm in front of the body (2), one stretching farther to the side, then stretch to position "1" (3), arms swinging down to the left to starting position (4), etc. Repeat to the opposite side.

7. Hip adbdominal exercise

Sitting, knees bent, feet off the floor, arms extended forward. Move the knees to the left, close to the floor, roll over on left hip (1), roll to the right, knees to the right (2), repeat (3-4), lie down on the floor, stretch the legs, arms along the sides, relax (5-6), rise to starting position (7-8).

8. Balance exercise

Standing, arms extended forward, shoulder distance apart. Raise left leg backward from the hip (1-2), raise higher while pushing the body forward to balance stand, back arched, left arm moving down, backward (3-6). Rise to starting position, raise upper part pulling the leg, (7-8). Repeat with the right leg.

9. Jump

(a) Moving sideways in mazurka rhythm, arms extended a little to the side. One hopping step to the left landing on left foot (1), right foot one step to the left crossing in front (2), hop on right foot, swinging left leg a little to the side, and clapping both feet together in the air, land on right foot (3), etc. Repeat to the right.

(b) As *a*, 3 times (1-3), (4-6), (7-9), 3 stamps on the spot, l.r.l. (10-12), repeat to the other side (1-12).

10. **Back exercise**

 (a) Lying on the stomach, arms extended forward, legs relaxed. Raise arms from the floor, bend upper back (1-2), to starting position, relax (3-4).

 (b) Bend your knees and catch the feet, pull knees and upper body off the floor, rock back and forth. "Rocking chair."

11. **Back, side exercise**

 Sitting, legs wide apart, hands on the back. Bend to the left, swinging right arm, to the side, up, touching left foot toes, left ear to left knee (1), 2 stretchings further and push (2-3) to starting position, right arm swinging up, sideways down (4). Repeat to the right side (5-8). Repetition. (See Program V, Exercise 12.)

12. **Abdominal exercise**

 Standing on feet and hands, straight body, right knee and hip stretched, left knee bent, left foot close to the hands, weight on hands. With light jumps change bending alternately left and right knee.

13. **Running**

 Running in waltz rhythm, arms extended forward, relaxing and stretching the arms and little bendings from side to side. When left foot starts, bend to the left, etc.

APPARATUS WORK

Balance beam
 (a) Repeat known exercises.
 (b) Make up a routine of known exercises.
 (c) Start training the headstands.

Tumbling
 (a) Handstand, forward roll.
 (b) Back extension.
 (c) Cartwheel.

Ropes
 (a) Climbing the ropes.
 (b) Each student two ropes, turn head upside down, standing between the ropes, make a "swallow's nest."

Vaulting box
 (a) (lengthwise) Free practice of known jumps.
 (b) (Crosswise) Free practice of known jumps.

PROGRAM XV

1. Free practice a few minutes, handstand, cartwheel.

2. **Running, walking**

   Walking in place, roll up on tiptoe and down on full foot, alternately left and right, little by little over to dipping, then prancing a little. Observe Footwork.

3. **Arm exercise**

   Standing, arms extended a little to the right. Swing the arms to the left, all the way up, down to the right in a big circle, relax and stretch back and knees (1), repeat twice (2-3), let the arms fall down and over to the left side, relax and stretch back and knees (4). Repeat the arms swing to the right 5-7, fall to the right (8), etc.

4. **Leg exercise**

   Standing, let the body fall forward, left foot a long step forward, arms extended to the sides (1), 2 bounces in the front knee (2-3), return to starting position, the back leg forward (4). Repeat with right foot (5-8), etc. (See Program XIII, exercise 3.)

5. **Back exercise**

   Standing, swing arms forward, relax and stretch the knees (1), continue raising the arms all the way up, stretching against the ceiling (2-4). (Try to make the whole body as long as possible.) Bend the upper back backward (5). 2 stretches (bounces) farther backward (6-7), raise and round the upper back a little forward, relaxing neck and knees, the arms falling forward, down, a little backward (8). The exercise now starts from this position, rolling up the back piece by piece, head and arms at last.

6. **Jump**

   Turn jump. 3 running steps moving forward, left, right, left, (1-3), on 3 swing right leg high up forward, jump straight up, turn 180° to the left (4). 2 hops in place, raising alternate knee (2 hops on each foot) (5-8). Repeat starting with the right foot.

7. **Side exercise**

   Standing, swing the arms forward, relax and stretch knees and back (1), turn to the left, swing the arms down, and backward on left side (2), hang backward and look at the back hand. Two stretchings farther backward, relax and stretch arms and knees, push the front hip forward (3-4). Turn, swing arms down forward to new 1, and repeat to the right. (See Program 8, exercise 4.)

8. **Abdominal exercise**

Lying on the back, arms extended to the side, roll over on left hip (1), to the right (2), repeat (3-4). Keep shoulders and feet on floor. Swing the legs to the left side, over to the right side drawing a lying figure-eight close to the floor (5-6), repeat (7-8).

9. **Back, Abdominal exercise**

Sitting, knees bent, feet off floor, one hand under each knee. Stretch the knees and touch the floor with toes and back to starting position, (1). Repeat twice (2-3) stretch the legs forward to long sitting and bend forward. Raise the feet high up, keep the back straight, lean back from the hips. Bend forward from the hips, one hand on each side of the *ankles* (4), one stretching farther forward (5), to starting position (6).

10. **Balance exercise**

Standing, arms extended forward, shoulder width apart. One step forward on left foot (1-2), right leg raising backward to balance stand, right arm moving down, backward (3-6). To starting position (7-8). Repeat on right foot.

11. **Jump**

Standing, 4 hops on right foot. Swing left leg backward on (1), forward, up (2), – to the right side crossing in front, touching the floor (3), to the left side close to the floor (4), 4 gallop jumps to the left (5-8). Repeat with right leg 1-4, 5-8.

12. **Back exercise**

Standing, straight back bent forward from hips, arms extended to the sides, move down and half up, swinging arms forward crossed in front of the chest (1-2), repeat (3-4), bend knees, relax back, neck and arms to tucked position, finger tips touching floor (5), roll up the back and stretch knees to standing position (6-8).

13. **Abdominal – side exercise**

On the knees sit on your heels. Rise to knee stand, swinging arms forward (1-2), lean backward from the knees, turn to the left, move left arm up and down, shoulder high (3-6), push from the floor with left hand, rise to knees and, left arm moving up (7). Arms fall forward, down, backward, sit on your heels, relax back and neck (8). Next time start from this position.

14. Mazurka

Repeat (a) One leaping step forward on left foot (1), — one on right (2), hop on right foot, raising left knee (3). Repeat leaping steps forward on right foot 1, etc. Several times.

(b) One high leaping step forward on right foot 4. 2 runnning steps 5-6, etc.

(c) Put *a* + *b* together. Once a (1-3), once b, (4-6), etc.

APPARATUS WORK

Balance Beam

(a) Free practice.

(b) Short runnning, take off on springboard, jump up on the end of the beam on one foot.

(c) Run and skip across beam.

(d) Cartwheel off the end of the beam.

Tumbling

(a) The take-off for running cartwheel, roundoff, handspring, etc. Hop and step — hop and step, etc.

(b) Running cartwheel. Start with 3-5 steps running.

Vaulting box

(Crosswise) Chest high, springboard, short running, take-off, head-spring. 3 spotters.

Buck (Crosswise)

Jump over the buck in squat position. Extend legs after clearing the buck.

PROGRAM XVI

1. Walking, running

Run in place, stress the footwork, little by little, raise the knee higher. over to flexible jumping.

2. Arm and back exercise

Standing position, arms extended upward. Bend upper back forward relaxed neck and knees, "question mark," and stretching up to starting position (1). Swing arms sideways down, forward, up, relax and stretch back and knees (2), bend upper back backward (3), stretch farther backward and up to starting position (4). (See Program 7, Exercise 4.)

3. Leg exercise

(a) From standing position: Step forward right, swing left leg forward, rolling up on tiptoe of right foot (1), swing left leg backward (dipping right knee and ankle) (2). Two steps forward, left, right. Left foot steps forward, right leg swinging, (3-4).

(b) As *a*, with flexible hops on (1-2-3).

(c) As *a* and *b*, moving 45° forward to the side. Starting with left foot, move to the right, left foot crossing in front.

4. Side exercise

Standing, feet apart, the weight on left foot, relaxed back, arms and left knee. Turn to the right, moving the weight over to the right foot. Left hip leads the movement, the arms are hanging relaxed and follow the movement passively (1), back to starting position (2), hold (3), (Waltz). Several times to the right. Repeat to the left side.

5. Jump

(a) Standing on the right foot, left leg extended low to the side. Hop on right foot moving to the left while clapping the feet together in the air on each jump 1, 2, etc.

(b) Standing, one leaping step to the left, left foot (1), right foot one step to the left crossing in front (2), one leap as *a* (3), continue moving to the left. Repeat to the right side. Mazurka- rhythm.

6. Back exercise

Standing, swing the arms forward, relax and stretch knees and back (1), bend forward, swing both arms down to the left and a little backward, relax neck, back and knees (2), swing the arms forward, stretch back and knees (3-4) (now bend forward from the hips, arms extended up, head up), relax arms, neck, back and knees (5), roll the back up to standing position (6-8). Repeat swinging the arms down on the right side (1-8).

7. Abdominal exercise

On your knees, sitting on your heels, rise to knee, standing position, swing the arms forward (1-2), bend backward from the knees, arched back (3-6), to knee stand, arms extended forward, with stretching upward (chest and arms like a wave) (7), arms falling down, then backward, sit on your heels, bend forward, relaxed neck and back (8). Next time start from this position.

8. Leg and back exercise

(a) Standing, step forward on left foot, moving the weight over, swing the arms forward, raise right leg a little backward from the hip (1), step backward on right foot, moving the weight over, raising the left leg a little forward, arms swinging down, backward, central back relaxed (2). 3 steps forward, left, right, left, hop on left foot; raise right knee, while swinging the arms forward up, and around in a big circle and forward up, around in a big circle and forward up (3-4), repeat, starting with right foot, arms swinging sideways down, forward, etc. (5-8).

(b) Standing, raise left leg backward to balance stand, arms forward (1-4), pause (5-6), raise upper part, keep the leg as high as possible (7), to standing position (8). Repeat raising right knee.

9. Jump

Three running steps moving forward, left, right, left, hop on the left, swing right leg high up forward (1-3), turn 180° to the left, (use the hips) (4). Hop in place on the right foot, raising left knee (5-6), repeat on left foot (7-8). The hop then starts with the right foot (1-8). Repetition (See program 15, exercise turn jump).

10. **Side exercise**

(a) Standing, arms extended upward. Swing the arms twice down to the right, sideways, up and around in a big circle, relax and stretch back and knees (1-2), bend to the right side, relaxing knees (3), stretch farther to the side (relax and stretch the arms, push left hip to the side, "sidewave"), to starting position (4). Repeat the armswing and bend to the other side (5-8).

11. **Abdominal exercise**

Sitting with bent knees, feet off the floor 3-4 inches, hands touching the floor outside the hips or extended forward, stretch the legs forward close to the floor, raise legs to balance seat (1-2). Bend knees to starting position (3), repeat (4-6), lie down on the back, stretch knees, relax (1-3), sit up to starting position (4-6).

12. **Back-side exercise**

Sitting with stretched legs wide apart, hands by the hips, relaxed arms, put left hand on floor just behind the hip, swing right arm forward up and rise on left hand and heels (1-2), sit down, swing both arms in a big circle forward to the right while bending forward (3), put right hand on floor; repeat, swinging left arm forward, up and rise on right hand and heels (4). Continue from side to side. Slow waltz rhythm.

13. **Walking**

Running, skipping to one or two lines along the wall.

14. **Back exercise**

"Bodywave." Step *a* and *b*. See supplemental material.

15. **Take-off**

For running cartwheel, round off and forward handspring. We here use left foot as "take-off-foot." One step forward with a hop on left foot raising right knee and swinging the arms forward, bend a little forward (1), step forward on right foot, swing the arms down backward (2). Count: hop! — step! 2-3 times, finish with a cartwheel.

APPARATUS WORK

Balance beam

(a) The students work on a routine made up by themselves.

(b) Stress the cartwheel down from the end of the beam.

(c) Headstand on the beam.

Vaulting box

Approximately chest high or a little lower, springboard. Headspring over the box.

Horse

(Crosswise) Jumping over the horse in squat position. Move the springboard little by little farther from the horse, approximately 1/2 yard, try to get the hips high.

Tumbling

(a) Running cartwheel.

(b) Forward roll, rise half on one foot, directly over to cartwheel.

PROGRAM XVII

1. Walking and running around the gym.

2. **Arm exercise**
   Standing, left armswing forward up, backward down in a big circle, ⊣ forward (1-2). Left armswing backwards up to a big circle backwards (3-4). All the way flexible movements in knees and central back. Continue with left arm. Repeat with the right.[10]

3. **Leg exercise**
   Standing, arms extended to the sides, shoulder high, left foot one step to the right, crossing in front, arms falling relaxed down, crossing the wrists in front, relax back. Keep the weight on left foot (1), right foot one step to the right, rise on tiptoe, stretching the back and raising the arms to the sides, raise left leg to the side (2), continue to the right; repeat to the left.

4. **Back exercise**
   (a) Standing, arms extended upward, bend upper back backward (1), one stretching deeper backward (2), deep bending backward, relaxed arms swing backwards, down, forward (3). Raise arms forward up, stretch back to the starting position (4).

5. **Scissors legs**
   Forward and backward. Start with left foot, one step forward, swing right leg forward, leap, swing left leg forward passing the right leg on the way down like a pair of scissors, land on right foot (1-2). Repeat with the legs swinging backward (3-4). Continue. Repeat starting with right foot, step forward.

6. **Side exercise**
   Standing, arms extended forward, shoulder high, shoulder width apart. Left arm swing down, backward, while turning the upper part to the left, hang backward, look at the back hand (1). Three stretchings, relax and stretch arms and knees, push the front hip forward, "sidewave" (2-4). Turn to the right, change arms, left arm swings down forward, right arm swings down backward (5), three stretchings (6-8). Repeat.

---

[10]Can be done with arms swinging backward first for body wave motion; swing backwards (1), forward (2), up and around (3), forward (4).

Fifteen year old girls from Real Secondary School, Valler, Norway, demonstrating Side Exercise

7. Abdominal exercise

Lying on the back, arms extended to the sides. Raise knees as close to the chest as possible keeping the whole back on floor (1), stretch the legs to the left side close to the floor (2-3), move the legs forward in a circle line close to the floor (4). Raise straight legs up, over the head, touching the floor behind the head (5-6), lower the legs to starting position (7-8). Repeat to the right side. (1-4), (5-8).

8. Back exercise

Long sitting, arms extended upwards. Bend forward turn to the left, stretch the arms down along the sides of the body, right arm forward, left arm backward close to the floor (1), stretch to starting position, arms rising sideways up (2-3), repeat turning to the right side (4-6).

9. Balance exercise

Standing, 2 steps forward, left, right (1-2), step forward on left foot with knee a little bent, rise on tiptoe, stretch the knee while swinging the right leg a little backward, up to the side in a high bow (3-4), repeat starting with right foot, swinging left leg (5-8). All the time keep the arms relaxed a little, extended to the sides or one arm high, see the drawing.

10. **Jump**

   Moving forward. Step forward on left foot, hop straight up while raising right knee (1-2), step forward on right foot, hop straight up raising the left leg a little backward, arch the back and look at the back
   leg (3-4), etc. Repeat starting the step with right foot.

11. **Hip, side exercise**

   Standing, feet wide apart, weight on left foot. Move the weight a little
   over to the right foot, bend both knees a little (1), push right hip to
   the right side, the upper part falling to the left side, (relax the neck)
   (2), stretch to starting position with the weight on right foot (3).
   Repeat to the opposite side (4-6). Slow waltz rhythm.

12. **Abdominal — back exercise**

   Standing on left knee, right leg extended forward, left arm to the
   side. Bend backward from the hips, slightly arched back, while raising
   right arm forward up (1-4), to starting position (5-8). Four to six
   times. Repeat on right knee.

13. **Back exercise**

   Standing on left knee as Exercise 12. Sit down on left heel, bend forward, stretch arms relaxed forward. Smooth bounces farther forward.
   Short duration. Repeat on right knee.

14. **Dancing-Steps**

   2 running steps forward (1-2), one jump on both feet, swing left leg a
   little backward, arched back, look at back leg, land on right foot (3-4),
   repeat with right leg swinging backward (5-8).

APPARATUS WORK

Balance beam

(a) Free practice.

(b) Stress the exercises from last program.

Vaulting box

Headspring. Move the springboard slightly farther from the box.

Horse

Practice the jump from last program. Try to get the hips high, keep
the back in 45° with the perpendicular line. Little by little stretch the
hips, swing the legs high up backward.

Tumbling

(a) Repeat last program.

(b) Make up a routine of headstand, handstand forward roll, diving forward, roll, jump 180° turn, backward roll with back extension, diving forward roll, headspring, diving forward roll, raise half up on one foot directly to cartwheel. Start combining 2 or 3 details, add one more at a time.

PROGRAM XVIII

1. Walking and running

2. Arm — leg exercise

(a) Repeat the running in waltz rhythm (1-3), (4-6), etc.

(b) Standing, arms extended to the sides. Bend upper part to the left, relax and stretch left arm, central back and knees (1-2-3), repeat to the right (4-5-6). "Sidewave."

(c) Put *a* and *b* together. Start the running with left foot when bending to the left, etc.

3. Back exercise

Standing, armswing forward, relax back and knees (1), swing arms down, sideways, up in a big circle with bodywave (2), arms fall forward, down, a little backward, relax back and knees (3). The exercise starts from this position (4-6), etc.

4. Back exercise

(a) Standing arms extended upward. Bend forward from the hips, head up, arched back (1-4), relax arms, neck, back and knees (the arms are falling by their own weight) (5), roll up (6-7), arms up to starting position (8). (b) As a, roll up on tiptoe while bending forward (1-4).

5. Abdominal — hip exercise

Lying on the back, arms extended to the sides. Raise left leg straight up (1), lower left leg to the right side, try to touch right hand (2), raise the leg to position (1) (3), — the leg down to starting position (4). Repeat with right leg. Keep shoulders on floor.

6. Jump

(a) Repeat exercise 10, Program XVII.

(b) Standing, turn 45° to the left from the moving direction, arms extended to the sides. Step forward with left foot crossing in front, hop on left foot, raise right knee, swing the arms down in front of the body, crossing the wrists, bend upper part a little forward, r e l a x n e c k,

rounded back (1-2), swing the arms out, raise the left leg a little backward (3-4), etc. Turn to the right, repeat starting with right foot crossing. Short steps forward, hop straight up, uneven rhythm: — and *hop* — and *hop!* etc.

7. Leg exercise

Standing, left leg swinging forward from the hip, backwards, high up forward, rise on tiptoe on right foot (1-3). Fall forward, landing on tiptoe on left foot, left knee bent, right leg stretched backward, hips straight over left heel, arms extended to the sides (4). (See Program XV, Exercise 3.) 3 bounces and stretch up standing on left foot, right leg extended backwards toes pointing to floor (5-8). Repeat with right leg (1-8), etc.

8. Balance exercise

Standing, arms extended forward, shoulder high, shoulder width apart. Step forward on left foot, relax and stretch arms, raise right leg a little backward from the hip (1-2), raise right leg farther backward to balance stand, arms pointing down toward the floor (3-4), move arms down backward, one on each side (5-6), relax standing knee, swing the arms down, forward, rise to starting position (7-8). Keep right leg extended backward ready for next step forward (1), etc. Repeat on the right foot (2-8).

9. Abdominal exercise

On the knees, sitting on heels, bend forward to tucked position. Swing arms forward up, rising to kneestanding position, (1). Bend backward from the hips slightly arched back (2). One stretch farther backward *and* stretching up to kneestand with arms extended up (3). Bend forward to starting position, arms falling relaxed forward down, backward (4).

10. Hip exercise

Standing on the knees, arms extended forward. Push hip to the left, sit down on left hip (1-2), return to starting position (3-4), repeat to the right (5-6), (7-8). Move from side to side without stopping. Little by little try to push the hips forward while rising to kneestand, so that the hips will be "drawing" a half circle forward.

11. Hop

(a) Step forward on left foot, make a hop raising right knee (right ankle extended) (1), raise left knee to the same height while right foot takes the floor (2). Keep on moving forward for a while. Prance like a pony.

(b) Same as *a*, moving to the side. Standing, arms extended a little to the sides. Raise left knee, knee turned 45° to the left, hop straight up, raise right knee turned 45° to the right, land on left foot (1), step on right foot crossing in front (2).

12. Side exercise

Standing arms extended upward. Bend to the left, relax knees (1), one stretch farther to the left *and* stretch up to starting position rising on tiptoe (2). Repeat to the right side (3-4). Continue from side to side without stopping. Waltz rhythm.

Eighteen year old girls from Real Secondary School, Valler, Norway, demonstrating Side Exercise

APPARATUS WORK

Balance beam

(a) Practice routines, jump up at the end of the beam, cartwheel down from the opposite side, move back and forth. Be sure to move steadily on the beam before turning.

(b) Start to practice handstand on the beam (to be used later on for handspring down). Beam approximately hip-high. Standing on the beam, lean forward, put hands on the beam and swing up to handstand sideways on the beam, shoulders parallel to beam (1/4 cartwheel). Spotter holding on hips, find the balance. Arch over and 1/2 twist, dismount.

Vaulting box

Headspring.

(a) Stress the jumping up from the springboard, hands on box first, then the forehead.

(b) Stress the stretching of the arms.

Horse

Continue practicing the jump, started in program XVI. Jump up with straight legs and the body in 45° with the perpendicular line. Push with the wrists and from the shoulders — bend from the hips and jump through.

Tumbling

(a) Continue the routine from last program.

(b) Stress the running cartwheel.

(c) Start the roundoff (See Tumbling, roundoff).

PROGRAM XIX

1. **Walking and running**

2. **Foot exercise**

   Standing, left leg extended backward, the
   front part of the foot on floor. Move down
   and up in the front knee stretching back
   ankle. Waltz rhythm. Smooth, flexible
   movements. Repeat with right leg extended
   backward.

3. **Arm exercise**

   Standing, left arm extended to the
   side, shoulder high. Swing left
   arm down, crossing in front of the
   body, to the right side, bending
   the upper part to the right, relax
   and stretch the knees (1). One
   stretch farther to the side, relax
   and stretch arm and knees, push
   hips to the left (2). Swing left arm

   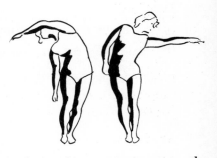

   down crossing in front and to the left, bending upper part to the
   left side (3). One stretch farther to the side (4). "Sidewave." Continue swinging and bending from side to side; the hip starts moving
   to the side. Repeat with the right arm.

4. **Back exercise**

   Standing, arms extended upward. Bend upper part forward, relaxed
   neck and knees, rounded back "question mark" (1). Dip smoothly
   in the back and knees and stretch to starting position (2). Bend upper back backward (3), one bending farther backward (4). Continue the exercise, bending back and forth nonstop. Waltz rhythm.

5. **Back exercise**

   Standing, swing arms forward, relax and stretch central back and
   knees (1). Bend forward from the hips, touch the floor far forward
   with the finger tips, while moving up and down from the hips (2-3).
   Swing arms down, backward, relax neck, back and knees (4). Swing
   arms forward, lead them up, to the sides while stretching the knees
   and straightening the back (5-6). (90° angle in the hips), the arms
   continue down along the sides of the body, swing forward, relax
   neck, back and knees, *and* rise to standing position, arms extended
   forward (7). Arms fall down, backward, relax knees and central
   back (8).

6. Hop

Standing, arms extended forward. 3 running steps, moving forward, left, right, left, arms swinging down, backward, one high hop straight up on left foot, raise right knee high, bend upper back forward, forehead against the knee. Arms swinging forward 1-2-3-4. Repeat starting with right foot 5-6-7-8

7. Balance — leg exercise

In couples, join inner hands. Swing outside leg forward, touch the floor with the toe and swing the leg high up to the side and backward in half circle (1). Touch the floor behind with the toes, swing the leg high up to the side and forward (2). Repeat 1 (3), touch the floor behind and raise back leg backward from the hip, rise high up on tiptoe (4). (All the time rolling up and down on the toes) — bend supporting knee, stretch the back leg backward along the floor (See Program XIII, Exercise 3) (5). Flexible movement in supporting knee, stretch to standing position (6-7). About face (8). Repeat with the other leg (1-8), etc.

8. Abdominal exercise

On the knees, sitting on your heels, upper back bent forward, relaxed neck, rounded back. Rise to kneestand, swing the arms forward up (1), lean backward from the knees, arched back, arms swinging backward, down, forward in a big circle (2). Bend farther backward swinging arms backward, up and rise to kneestand, arms extended up (3), bend to starting position, arms falling forward down, backward (4).

9. Back — side exercise

Longsitting, arms extended forward. Left armswing down backward, turn to the left (1). Touch the floor far behind (push), swing left arm to the side, up, turn forward (2). Bend forward, one hand on

each side of the feet (3). One stretch farther forward *and* return to starting position (4). Repeat with the right arm, turning to the right (5-8).

10. **Abdominal — leg exercise**

    Lying on the back. Stretch the legs along the floor, make them as long as possible (1), raise the legs, toes pointing toward the ceiling (2-4), relax lower leg, bend knees, legs falling down by their own weight (5-6). Relax upper leg to starting position (7-8). Repetition.

11. **Abdominal — hip exercise**

    Sitting, both legs to the left side, left leg straight, right knee bent, arms extended forward. Swing the legs forward with bent knees (1), stretch to balance seat (2). Swing the legs to the right (3), stretch right leg (4). Repeat to the other side (5-8). Repetition.

12. **Leap**

    (a) From stand leap forward, land on left foot (toes), keep right leg extended backward, lean forward (1). Leap backward landing on right foot (2). Repeat (3-4), (5-6), 3 running steps, moving forward (7-8). Repeat with right foot forward (1-8).

    (b) As *a*, move diagonally 45° to the left when left foot is in front, 45° to the right when right foot is in front.

13. **Balance exercise**

    Standing, arms extended forward. Raise left leg backward from the hip, left arm up, look at the hand, arch the back (*1*-2), raise the leg farther backward, lower the arm halfway down to the side, backward to balance stand (3-6), relax standing knee, swing left arm down forward, rise to starting position (7-8). Repeat with right arm and leg (1-8).

14. **Side exercise — hop**

    (a) Standing, arms extended a little to the sides. Moving to the left, right foot one step to the left, crossing in front, raise left knee, turned 90° to the left, hop on right foot (*1*-2), stretch left leg to the side, push the hips to the left (3). Step to the left on left foot (4). Continue several times to the left. Repeat to the right.

    (b) As *a*, when stretching the left leg to the side, let the body fall relaxed to the right, stretch up on 4.

    (c) As *b*, more speed, counting *1* — 2 —. Arms falling down crossing in front on 1, swinging out to the sides, shoulder high 2.

APPARATUS WORK

Balance beam

(a) Practice different jumps on the beam.

(b) Round off down from the end of the beam.

(c) Shoulderstand.

(d) Balance seat, swing legs on each side of beam backward up to squat position.

(e) Stress the routine from last programs.

Vaulting box

Lengthwise. Jump up on the box to squat position, put your hands on the farthest end, make a handstand, arch over, push away with the hands and land on the mat. (The second part of handspring over the vaulting box.)

Horse

Stress the jump from last program.

Tumbling

(a) Practice the round off. First standing, then with take off, one, two — three steps and little by little full run.

(b) Start handspring, step *1* and *2*.

(c) Snap, step 1.

PROGRAM XX

1. **Walking, running**

2. **Arm exercise**

   Standing, feet apart, weight on left foot, left arm extended to the side. Left armswing down, crossing in front to the right, moving the weight over on right foot (1), one stretch farther to the right, "sidewave" (2). Left armswing down crossing in front to the left, moving the weight over on left foot (3), one stretch farther to the left (4). Continue from side to side, the hip leading the movement. Repeat with right arm (See Program 19, Exercise 3).

3. **Leg exercise**

   Standing, armswing forward, relax and stretch back and knees (1), armswing down sideways out, rising on tiptoe (2), fall forward, long step forward, landing on left foot, weight on left foot. (See Program XIII, Exercise 3). Arms falling forward down, a little backward (3). Swing the arms forward up, sideways down in a big circle dipping in front knee (4). Arms swing forward, dipping in front knee *and* rising to stand on left foot, arms extended forward (5). Feet closed, arms falling down, a little backwards, relax and stretch back and knees (6). Repeat on right foot (1-6), etc.

4. **Back exercise**

   (a) Standing with arms extended upward. Bend upper part forward, relax neck and knees, "question mark" (1), dip upper back and knees smoothly (2), bodywave, arms swinging down, sideways up (3)! One stretch farther backward (4).

   (b) Twice exercise *a*, (1-4), (5-8), bend forward from the hips, arch the back, look up, keep the arms extended upwards (1-4), relax arms, neck, back and knees (5), roll up the back (6-7), stretch the arms to starting position (8). (See Program XVIII, Exercise 4.)

5. **Jump**

   Step forward on left foot, swing right leg high forward, jump on left foot and turn 180° "turn jump" (1). 2 steps: right, left, (2-3), stepping on right foot backwards, swinging left leg down backwards.

Jump and turn 180° to the left (4). Two steps forward left, right
(5-6). Continue in the same direction all the time. Waltz rhythm.
Repeat starting with right foot.

6. Back exercise

Standing, armswing forward,
relax and stretch back and
knee (1), bend forward from
the hips, touch floor with the
finger tips far forward moving a little up and down
from the hips (2-3). Swing

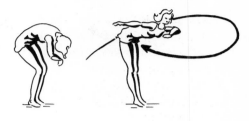

arms relaxed down, backward on left side, relax neck, back and knees
(4). Dipping your knees, swing the arms forward (5), stretch the
back, stretching arms far forward and to the right side (6). Relax
neck, back and knees and stretch up, swing arms forward (to standing
position, arms extended forward) (7). The arms fall down, a little
backward; relax and stretch back and knees (8). Repeat with the
arms swinging to the other side. *Obs.* Bend back straight forward,
no turn.

7. Side exercise

(a) Standing, arms extended upward. Repeat sidebending, relaxing,
the knees (1). One stretch farther to the side and stretching up to
starting position. Rise on tiptoe (2). Repeat to the other side. (See
Program XVIII, Exercise 12.)

(b) Jump a short step to the left, land on left foot, put right foot fast
behind left foot, relaxed knees (toes on both feet turned 45° to the
side, weight on left foot) (1), dip (2), repeat to the right (3-4).

(c) Put *a* + *b* together. Jump to the side while bending to the same
side, etc.

8. Abdominal exercise

Standing on left knee, right leg extended forward, foot on floor, arms
along the sides. Raise arms forward up, while bending backward from
the hips and leaning to the right, (1-4). Raise and lower the arms forward, down to starting position (5-8). Continue leaning to the right.
Repeat standing on right knee, leaning to the left.

9. Stretching exercise

Sitting in "hurdle" position, bend forward between the legs. Arms
stretched forward, look forward, small, smooth stretches forward. Short

duration. Repeat with the other leg bent. Shake the legs. Repetition (See Program XII, Exercise 12).

10. **Balance — leg exercise**

(a) 2 steps forward, left, right (long, short) (*1*-2), step forward on left foot, keeping the whole foot on floor roll up on tiptoe swing right leg sideways up in a circle (3-4), repeat starting with right foot, swinging left leg (5-6), (7-8).

(b) As *a*, swinging the arms to the side, left arm continue up, right arm follow the leg in a circle forward (3-4). Lower the arms forward down on (*1*-2).

(c) As *a*, the arms extended a little to the sides, flexible jump on (3). Repetition (See Program XVII, Exercise 9).

11. **Abdominal exercise**

Lying on the back, arms relaxed along the sides, knees bent, feet on floor. Raise hips from the floor, standing on feet, shoulders and head, hips stretched (1-4), roll down to starting position, beginning with shoulders, upper back, middle back, lower back, and hips (5-7), relax (8).

12. **Running steps**

Standing, arms extended to the sides, run 6 steps forward, raise knee high, start with left foot (1-6). Run 6 steps in a circle, left foot forward a little to the side (1), right foot step backward crossing to the left (2), left foot step backward (3), right foot forward to the side (4), left foot step forward crossing to the right (5), right foot step forward (6). Continue building the circle to the left. Repeat starting with right foot, building the circle to the right.

APPARATUS WORK

Balance beam

Make up an individual routine lasting from 1:15 — 1:45.

Vaulting box

(a) Handspring over a low box, approximately hip-high.

(b) Handspring over a box of normal height.

(c) Springboard farther from the box.

(d) Practice the handspring on the horse.

Tumbling

Continue the handspring.

Supplemental Material

SECTION TWO

SUPPLEMENTAL MATERIAL

Strengthening, stretching, posture and warming-up exercises. The following exercises are meant as supplemental material to the other programs. They are useful as warming up before apparatus work, basic for separate training with posture, stretching and strengthening which is of great importance. They can be used by performers at all ages if only starting with the simpler exercises and following the progression. Use the following exercises in every program, some one week (month), others next week (month), repeat them again and again. At the same time stress right breathing using the diaphragm. A few of these exercises will be found in the programs I-XX.

1. Feet and leg exercises

(a) Students lined up along the wall, right side to the wall, touching it with right hand for balance. Swing left leg forward, backward with relaxed leg. Keep the knee a little bent. Little by little swing higher up forward. Turn, and repeat with right leg.

(b) Starting position as *a*, left foot resting behind the right, toes pointing to the left. Swing left leg straight to the side and down to starting position. Turn, and repeat with right leg.

(c) Standing position as *a*, left leg extended to the side, pointed toe on the floor. Swing left leg to the right, crossing in front of right leg, bent knee, swing left leg down to the left side, keep the knee bent and turn the knee to the left. The lower leg and foot are hanging relaxed, the foot touching the floor in every swing. Turn and repeat with right leg.

(d) Starting position as *c*, swing left leg to the right with bent knee, down to the left with straight leg. Turn and repeat with right leg.

(e) Students lined up along the wall, facing the wall. Stand on tiptoe with the feet together, hands on the wall for balance. "Kick" up and down (down and up) only flexing the ankles, heels touching the floor for a moment, then back on tiptoe. Count: down — up! — down — up! When finished shake your legs.

(f) Same exercise as *e*, standing on one foot, the other knee slightly raised. Repeat with the other foot. Shake legs.

(g) Standing on one foot, the other leg extended forward, arms extended forward or one hand on the wall for balance. Bend your knee on standing leg, and stretch up. Down — up! Start bending just a little, then go deeper. When strong enough, the students should afford 4-6 times all the way down and up

(h) Squat position, arms extended forward. Swing arms backward, forward up with a high jump straight up, arch the back, head up, look at the hand, land in starting position.

2. **Arm and shoulder exercise**

(a) Standing by the stallbar (if stallbars are not available, use the beam, vaulting box, etc.) facing the bar. Place the wrists on the bar approximately shoulder high, bend forward and move backwards to get the legs straight in 90° angle with the floor, arms stretched, feet a little apart. Move shoulders down to stretch the pectoralis major. Smooth, slow movements down and up, no jerking, count: down–down! etc.

(b) Sitting with legs crossed, arms extended to the side a little higher than shoulder high, palms forward. Move the arms backward, pull the back muscles. Keep the back straight, shoulders low and head up Count: back —and — back — and. . .

(c) Standing on hands and feet, straight body. Flex the hips, move the chest against the legs and stretch farther. Count: back —and — back — and —

(d) Modified push-ups. Standing on knees and hands, bend the arms, chest to the floor, head up, and stretch up to starting position.

(e) Starting position as d, move the hands farther forward, move the weight over the arms. Bend and stretch the arms, chest to floor, head up.

(f) "Push-ups." Standing on hands and feet, body straight. Bend and stretch arms, chest to the floor. Down — up! A fairly good student can do 4-6 "push-ups" all the way down and up.

3. **Back exercises**

(a) Sitting with the legs crossed, one hand resting on each knee, relaxed arms. Relax central back, (keep the head up all the time) like the air going out of a balloon (1-2), stretch from lower back piece by piece (3-4). Try to get the back as long as possible, keep shoulders down, relaxed.

(b) Lying on the stomach, relaxed legs, arms along the sides. Bend backwards (upper back) (1-2), and down to starting position (3-4). Raise the head a little, but avoid tightening the shoulder blades.

(c) Lying on the stomach, one hand under each shoulder. Raise head, keep the hips on floor (1-4), down to starting position piece by piece, head at last (5-8). Last time stop on count 4, bend your knees, press the toes against the head.

(d) On the knees, sitting on your heels, bend forward with rounded, relaxed back, relaxed arms along the legs, hand pointing backwards. Stretch the back forward, look up and arch the back (1-4), roll down to starting position, relax (5-8).

(e) Starting position as *d*, back straight up, arms along the sides. Stretch arms down (make them longer) arch the back and look up, lean forward from the hips to 45° angle (1-4), relax arms, back and neck, roll to starting position from lower back, head at the end (5-8). When the students are doing this quite well, put more speed on and finish by a waving movement in waltz rhythm. The movement gets smaller the faster exercise is done.

(f) Lying on the stomach, feet under the lowest bar (if no stallbar, work in couples, the one doing the exercise, the other on her knees holding the performer's feet). Arms along the sides, hands behind the neck or arms extended upwards, depending on the flexibility and strength of the student's back. Bend backwards as high as possible, moderate speed. Up! and down! 4-6 times, then 4-6 times with more speed.

Girls from Real Secondary School, Valler, Norway, demonstrating Back Exercise

(g) *Bodywave.*

1) Standing by the wall (stallbar), facing the wall, hands on the bar (wall), chest high. Relax knees and central back, push hips and knees forward, bend the head and upper back relaxed backward (1),

stretch up, head at last (2), relax knees and central back (3). Start again from this relaxed position. Waltz rhythm.

2) Standing by the wall, left side to the wall, left hand on the bar (wall). Swing right arm forward, relax knees and central back (1) dipping your knees, push hips and knees forward, bend head and upper back relaxed backward, swing right arm down, backward, up and stretch (2), right arm continues the big circle forward down and a little backward, relax knees and central back (3). Start from this position, keep the relaxed position while swinging the arm forward, etc. About face, and repeat with left arm.

3) Same as 2) rising on tiptoe.

(h) Standing on knees and hands, tighten the lower back muscles, make a little swayback (bend the joint between the lumbar vertebrae and sacrum((1-2), tighten the lower abdomen muscles and round the same part of the back.

(i) Starting position as *h*. Move the lower back (same part as *h*) smoothly to the left (1-2), to the right (3-4). Obs! Keep the weight on both knees all the time!

4. Relaxing exercises for shoulder and neck

(a) Standing, relaxed arms along the sides, raise shoulder high, let them fall relaxed down (1-2).

(b) Starting position as *a*. Move the shoulders up, backward, down in a circle.

(c) Sitting with legs crossed, one hand on each knee, bend the head straight to the left, stretching the right side (1-2), bend to the right side (3-4), move slowly from side to side.

(d) Starting position as *c*. Let the head fall relaxed forward (1-2), stretch up from vertebrae prominent, trying to make the backside long.

(e) As *d*. Bend the head backward from vertebra prominent (1-2), to starting position (3-4).

(f) Starting position as *c*. Roll the head in a half circle, forward to the left, backward, up (1-4), repeat to the right (5-8). Relax neck muscles.

(g) Standing on knees and hands, straight back, long neck. Let head fall relaxed forward down (1-2), stretch up to starting position, backside long (3-4).

5. Stretching exercise for lower leg and hamstrings

(a) Squat position, the whole foot on floor, arms extended forward. Small, smooth dips down and very little up, trying to push the knees forward and hips down.

(b) Standing facing the wall, approximately 1 yard's distance from the wall, lean forward hands on wall, left knee bent, roll up on tiptoe, stretch right knee and try to get right heel close to the floor. Change all the time with a cycling movement, stretching and bending alternate leg (1-2), etc.

(c) Standing on hands and feet, body straight (starting position as for "push-ups"), move shoulders backward bending the hips, bend left knee and roll left foot over on the front part of ankle, stretch right heel close to floor. Change bending right knee and roll over on front part of right foot (1). Change to left (2). Keep on bending and stretching alternate knee and ankle with a cycling movement.

(d) Longsitting, facing the stallbar (wall) feet to lowest bar (wall), stretched knees, back straight, arms extended forward. Lean forward from the hips, try to catch the third or fourth bar (or hands touching the wall). Small, smooth stretches farther forward. Shake the legs.

6. Strengthening exercises for upper leg, hipbenders and abdominal muscles

(a) Lying on the back. Raise upper part 1/2 up, approximately 45° starting with the head, rounded back (1-4), down to starting position, head at last, relax (5-8).

(b) Lying on the back. Raise upper body, bend the knees, feet off the floor, head against the knees (1-4), down to starting position, relax.

(c) Lying on the back, knees bent, feet on floor a little apart. Raise upper part, start with the head, rounded back, head against the knees (1-4), back to starting position, head the last (5-8).

(d) As c with the hands behind the neck, elbows to the side.

(e) Lying on the back, feet between third and fourth bar, 90° angle in knees and hips, arms along the side. Raise upper part, head against the knees, rounded back (1), down to starting position (2), the first times fairly slow, then more speed.

(f) As e, hands behind the neck, elbows to the side.

(g) Strengthening the front thighs. On the knees, sitting on your heels leaning a little backward, arms extended forward. Stretch hips, push the hips forward, (1-2), back to starting position.

(h) Hanging in the highest bar (stallbar, beam) back to the wall. Raise left knee high up, (1), down (2), right knee up (3), down (4).

(i) As *h*, raise both knees (1), down (2). Try to get the knees up to the chin, round back. Little by little put more speed on.

(j) As *h*, raise both knees (1), stretch the knees (toes pointing to the ceiling if possible) (2), lower the knees slowly (3-4).

(k) As *h*, raise both legs with stretched knees, up (1) — down (2).

(l) Strengthening exercise for gluteal muscles and backside of thighs, lying on the stomach, knees bent a little apart, cross your arms in front, head on arms, raise one knee (1-2), down (3-4), the other (5-6), (7-8).

(m) As *l*, raise both knees (1-2), down (3-4).

(n) As *l*, raise both knees (1), stretch the legs high up backward (2), lower the legs to the floor (3), to starting position (4).

Girls from Real Secondary School, Valler Norway, demonstrating strengthening exercises for Upper Leg, Hiphenders and Abdominal Muscles

7. Side exercises

(a) Lying on left side, left arm extended up on the floor, head on the arm, right hand on the floor in front of the chest, straight knees and hips. Raise right leg high up to the side (1), down to starting position, (2).

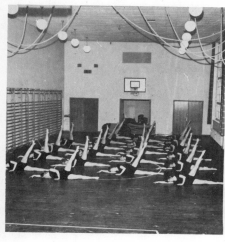

Girls from Real Secondary School demonstrating Side Exercises

(b) As *a,* raising both legs at a time (1), down to starting position (2). Repeat on right side.

(c) Lying on the side, both arms extended upward, one foot under, and one over lowest bar (if bars not available work in pairs, the one standing on her knees holding the other's ankles). Raise upper part straight to the side (1-2), down to starting position, relax (3-4).

(d) Standing by the stallbar, left side to the wall, left foot on the fourth bar, left hand hanging relaxed in front of left leg, right arm extended upward. Bend straight to the left, relax right arm hanging long over the head. Small stretches farther to the side. Repeat to the other side.

(e) Starting position as *d.* Arms extended upward. Bend straight to the left (1-4), turn to the left, 4 smooth stretches farther forward down (5-8), turn back to sidebending and stretch up to starting position (1-2), bend straight to the right side (3-4), turn to the right, 4 smooth relaxed stretches farther down (5-8), turn to sidebending, stretch up, etc. bending from side to side. Repeat to the other side.

(f) Standing with left side close to the bar, feet "under" the lowest bar. Catch the bar close to the ear (shoulder) with right hand, move left hip to the side, hang in a bowline, head relaxed against the shoulder. Move hips carefully farther to the side with small, smooth stretchings, short duration. Repeat to the other side.

Eighteen year old girls from Real Secondary School, Valler, Norway, demonstrating Side Exercise

Eighteen year old girls from Real Secondary School, Valler, Norway, demonstrating Side Exercises

8. Hip exercise

Standing, left side to the wall, left hand on the wall for balance, raise right knee, catch right heel with right hand on the innerside, bending left knee 1. Stretch right leg forward up 2. Move right leg to the side, stretching left knee 3, lower right leg slowly down 4-6. Repeat with left leg.

Demonstration Program

SECTION THREE

DEMONSTRATION PROGRAM

BEGINNERS

1. On one line, join hands, right arm forward, left arm backward, run to a circle with small steps. Stop, drop the hands, turn 180° and walk 1-2 steps forward.

2. **Arm exercise**

   Standing, armswing forward, backward (1-2), twice forward up, out, down, in a circle (3-4), relax knees and back, and stretch, repeat 3 times, (5-8), (1-4), (5-8). Last time stop with arms a little to the side. Directly over to:

3. **Leg exercise**

   Standing, left leg swings forward, backward, forward (1-3), bend standing knee and stretch (4). Repeat with the right leg (5-8), a small jump forward, down to squat position with rounded back, finger tips on the floor, bounce knees 3 times (1-4), stretch up. Head at last (5-7), turn 180° (to the left) (8). Repeat (1-8), (1-8). When turning the last time, stretch arms forward. Directly over to:

4. **Back exercise**

   Standing with arms extended forward, raise left arm while bending upper back backwards (1-2), to starting position (3-4). Bend forward from the hips, touch the floor far forward twice (5-6), swing the arms backward, relax neck, back and knees. Dip the knees, moving arms forward and stretch up to starting position (7-8). Repeat with right arm (1-4), (5-8). Directly over to:

5. **Side exercise**

   Standing with arms extended forward, swing both arms down on the left side, twist upper body to the left, relax knees and lean backwards, look at the hands (1). Swing arms down, forward and turn back to starting position (2). Repeat to the right (3-4), to the left (5-6), to the right with one step backwards and turn 180° (7). Swing arms down to the sides and up, and join hands on (8).

6. **Jump**

   4 running steps on tiptoe, to the left, around the circle, bend the back forward, bent knees (1-4), 4 running steps with arms extended up, stretched and arched back, look over front hand (5-8). Turn 90° facing the center of the circle and jump on left foot, raise right knee (1-2), repeat with left knee raised (3-4), repeat (5-6), (7-8). Repeat the whole exercise to the right.

7. **Hip and back exercise**

   Standing, join hands, raise left leg backwards, stretched knee and
   ankle (1-2), swing left leg forward up (3), and down to starting position (4). Repeat with the right (5-8), left and right (1-4), (5-8). On
   the last 8, drop hands and turn 90° to the left.

8. **Abdomen, thigh exercise**

   Bend knees to squat position (1-2), on the knees (3), sit on your heels
   (4), bend forward, rounded back (5-6). Raise to knee standing, move
   left arm in a circle forward, to the side, turn palms up (1-3), bend
   backward and turn to the left, touch the floor far behind the feet (4-6),
   stretch and turn forward, move the arm to the side (1-3), down to
   starting position (4-6), repeat to the right (1-6), (1-6), repeat (1-6),
   (1-6), (1-6), (1-6). On the last (4-6), move right leg to the side, foot
   on floor (4-5), left arm extended to the side, shoulder high (6).
   Directly over to:

9. **Side abdomen exercise**

   (a) Standing on left knee, right leg to the side, foot on floor, left arm
   extended to the side, swing left arm down, in front of the body (1),
   out, up (2). Bend to the right side and stretch (3-4), repeat (5-8, 1-4),
   on next (5-8) push left hip to the side and sit with stretched knees,
   turn 90° to the right (5-6), lie down on the back (7-8).

   (b) Lying on the back, rise half up with rounded back (1-2), down
   (3-4), repeat (5-6, 7-8). Raise upper body, bending your knees,
   rounded back, arms forward (1-4), turn 90° to the right and stand on
   your knees (5-6), left leg to the side (7), right arms extended to the
   side (8). Repeat *a* + *b*. On last (5-8), lie down on the back (5-6), turn
   leftward on the stomach with the arms extended forward (7-8).
   Directly over to:

10. **Back exercise**

    (a) Lying on the stomach, with the arms extended forward, raise
    arms, head and upper back (1-2), down to starting position (3-4), re-
    peat (5-6, 7-8).

    (b) One hand under each shoulder, bend backward, stretch the arms
    (1-4), down (5-8). Cross arms, head on the arms. Directly over to:

11. **Hip exercise**

    Lying on the stomach with the arms crossed, head on the arms, raise
    left leg backward (1), cross and touch the floor on right side (2),
    raise the leg (3), down to starting position (4). Repeat with right leg,
    (5-8), repeat left and right (1-4, 5-8). On last (6-8), turn to sitting
    position with legs apart, hand on the back. Directly over to:

12. **Back, side, abdomen exercise**

Sitting with legs apart, hands on the back. Swing right arm to the side up, bend towards left leg, left ear on left knee (1), stretch and touch the toes twice (2-3), on 3 push and stretch up, swing right arm up, arm down to starting position (4). Repeat to the right with left arm (5-8), repeat (1-4, 5-8). On 8, legs together, bend forward from the hips, arms extended forward (1), stretch (3) times (2-4), relax the back and roll down to lying position (5-8). Raise stretched legs up and backward, touch the floor behind the head (1-4), swing the legs forward up to standing position in couples facing each other (5-8).

13. **Jump**

Hop in place on right foot, bend left knee, foot behind right knee (1), stretch left leg to the side, down (2), 2 jumps with closed feet (3-4). Repeat with right leg (5-8), clasp hands, join hands while jumping 4 gallop steps to the side (1-4), four jumps on the spot with closed feet (5-8), repeat and gallop to the opposite side (1-8, 1-8). Repeat (1-8), (1-8), (1-8), (1-8). On the last 8, turn 90° to the right and join inner hands. Skip out.

ADVANCED GYMNASTS

1. Marching in the middle of the gymnasium on 4 lines, walking on the spot, running in place, and jumping.

2. **Arm, side exercise**

Standing, left armswing down cross over to the right with a little sidebending to the right (1), one stretching with sidewave (2), left armswing down, cross to the left, bending to the left (3), one stretch with sidewave (4). Left armswing down in front of the body (5), — sideways up in a circle (6), down to the left (7), stretching with sidewave (8). Repeat with right arm (1-8), repeat (1-8, 1-8). Directly over to:

3. **Back exercise**

Swing both arms forward while turning 45° to the left (1), raise left arm while bending upper back backward (2), bend deeper and stretch up (3), bend upper back forward, relax knees and swing arms down backward (4). Repeat with right arm from this position (5-8). Repeat both sides (1-4), (5-8). Directly to:

4. **Side exercise**

Swing both arms forward while stretching up the back, swing left arm down and backward, twist to the left, look at left hand, lean backward (2), 2 stretches with sidewave (3-4). Change arms, left arm down forward, right arm down backward and twist to the right (5), 3 stretchings with side-wave (6-8). Repeat (1-4, 5-8). On the last 8, move both arms up and turn forward. Directly over to:

5. Back exercise (forward)

(a) Standing with the arms extended up, bend forward from the hips (1-4), relax and roll up (5-8).

(b) Swing arms forward, relax and stretch knees and central back (1). Bend forward, touch the floor far forward with finger-tips. Swing arms backward, relax neck, back and knees (3), bounce your knees swinging the arms forward, up, out and down (circle) while stretching up (4). Repeat twice. Turn 45° to the right.

6. Jump

Standing, hop 4 times on right foot, left leg swinging backward, forward, up, down crossing right foot and touching the floor, out on left side touching the floor (1-4), 4 slidesteps to the left (5-8). 4 jumps forward, bending forward and stretching up while the arms move forward up (1-4). 4 jumps backward, arms moving sideways down (5-8). On 8, jump with closed feet. Repeat with right leg swinging, slide to the right.

7. Balance

In couples, join innerside hands. Raise left leg backward while moving both arms forward up, arch the back (1-2), to balance stand, arms moving forward down (3-4), move arms backward (5-6) to starting position, swing the arms down forward (7-8). Repeat with right leg (1-8). Repeat (1-8, 1-8). Directly over to:

8. Leg exercise

Standing in couples, join innerside hands. Left legs swinging forward, backward twice, rising on tiptoe (1-4), bend standing knee, left leg extended backward on the floor (5), bounce (6-7), to starting position (8). Repeat with right leg (1-8), repeat (1-8, 1-8). On last 6-8 move down on back knee (6). On both knees (7), sit on your heels (8). Directly over to:

9. Abdomen, thigh exercise

Swing arms forward, rise to kneestand (1-2), swing left arm down backward, turning to the left (3-4), bend backward (5-7), on 7, push from the floor, swing left arm up and turn forward, bend forward, sit on your heels, swinging arms down and backward (8). Bounce knee and hips, and return to kneestand, repeat turning to the right

(3-8). Repeat (1-8, 1-8). On the last 8, sit down to the left, knees bent, hands on the floor by the hips, turn 45° to the right. Directly over to:

10. Abdomen exercise

Sitting with bent knees. Stretch your legs forward close to the floor (1-2), raise them (3), bend your knees (4), repeat (5-8). Lie down on the back, stretching your knees (1-4), rise to starting position (5-8). Repeat (1-8, 1-8). On last (5-8), sit up with stretched knees. Directly over to:

11. Back exercise

Sitting with stretched knees, hand on the back, bend forward and stretch left arm swinging forward to the right and left in an figure-eight movement (1-2), stretch forward, up, left arm swinging rightward up, sideways down to starting position (3-4). Repeat with right arm (5-8). Repeat with both arms (1-4), place right hand on the floor, turn and jump up on the feet (5-8).

12. Side exercise

Standing with the arms extended up, bend to the left (right) (1), deeper bending (2), another deep bending, dropping left (right) arm down in front of the body (3), swing left arm sideways up while stretching to starting position (4). Repeat to the right (left) (5-8). Repeat (1-4, 5-8). On the last 8, put your hand on your partner's shoulder.

13. Jump

Standing, feet 90° angle, left heel to the right big toe. A small jump to the left, land on toes — heel, (1). Raise right knee, right foot behind the left (starting position) (2). Repeat (3-4-5-6). Two hops on left foot, bend and stretch right leg downward, always pointing 45° to the right (7-8). Repeat to the right (1-8). Move forward, 2 hops on each foot, hop on left foot, raise right knee turned 45° to the right, foot behind left knee (1-4), one hop on each foot (5-8). Move backward, 2 hops on each foot, knee raised forward (1-8). Repeat (1-8, 1-8, 1-8, 1-8).

Exercises With Rhythm Balls

SECTION FOUR

EXERCISES WITH RHYTHM BALLS

The exercises with balls are supposed to be a play with balls, the ball being mostly in the air.

Take notice of the following from the very beginning:

1) Do not grasp at the ball; the ball is meant to be resting in the slightly bent fingers.
2) The whole body takes part in the movement and follows the ball closely. When the ball throws upward, stretch the body; when the ball is on its way down, catch it with a smooth, flexible movement, relaxing central back and knees.
3) Do not be afraid of losing the ball. Always work with relaxed muscles, avoid stiffening. Take special care of arm and shoulder muscles, relax face muscles as well. In the beginning, rather lose the ball, doing the movements correctly, than trying to keep on the ball.

When starting the exercises, let the students move about freely with the ball to get familiar with it. Also let the students follow different kinds of music moving around, separately making up their own exercises. They have to move up and down, jump, bounce the ball, turn, run, etc.

PROGRAM I

1. (a) Standing with feet together, arms extended to the sides, shoulder height, the ball in the right hand. Small throw with the back and knees relaxing and stretching. "The body throws." Look at the ball. Repeat with left hand.

   (b) Standing as *a*. Move the ball behind the back to the left hand; the hips follow the ball. Bend a little in the knees and push the hips to the left at the same time as the ball rolls from the right to the left hand (Count 1) to starting position, stretch up (Count 2). The opposite way (Count 3-4).

   (c) Combine *a and b*. 3 throws with right hand (Count 1-3) move the ball behind the back as *b* (Count 4), 3 throws with the left hand (Count 1-3), move the ball to the right hand as *b* (Count 4) and so on.

2. **Throw forward, up, the ball in both hands**

   The ball rests in the hands and against the wrist in front of the chest, bent elbows.

   (a) Stretch the arms up, a little forward, stretch knees, hips and upper back, the ball rolls to the finger tips (Count 1), the ball rolls back to starting position, relax back and knees (Count 2).

   (b) Same as *a* with throw. In the beginning low throws, then higher and higher. Catch the ball as high up as possible and relax as *a*.

3. **Throw under the knee**

   Standing as Exercise 1. Throw the ball with the right hand under the left knee (Count 1). Catch the ball with the left hand to starting position (Count 2). Raise the knees high up, bend standing knee and round the back. At the beginning roll the ball from one hand to the other, then small throws, and then the full throw.

Girls from Real Secondary School, Valler, Norway, demonstrating exercises with Rhythm Balls

4. Throw over the head

(a) Standing with the feet together, arms extended to the sides, the ball in the right hand, bend a little to the right side, relaxed knees and back. Move the ball sideways up and change it over to the left hand as high as possible over the head, arms down to starting position with a small side bending to the left and relaxing. The throw starts from waistline, swing the arm and ball up.

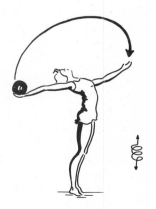

(b) Same as *a* with throw.

5. Bounce the ball

(a) Standing with feet together, right arm extended forward a little to the side, the ball rests in the hands. Turn palm down and bounce the ball, relax the back and knees when the ball goes down, stretch when the ball moves up. "Bounce with the whole body."

(b) As *a* with hop in place, alternate knee raising.

6. Throw straight up

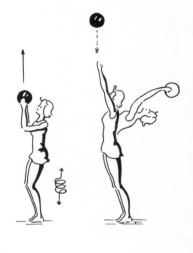

Standing with the feet together, the ball rests on the lower part of the hand, the fingers straight up and touch the ball loosely, the elbows are relaxed down.

(a) Throw the ball straight up with stretching, catch the ball as high as possible to starting position with relaxed back and knees (Count 1-2).

7. Upper back exercise

Starting position as 6. Stretch the arms upward and backward with back bending backward, look at the ball (Count 1-2) stretch up with the arms extended up (Count 3) to starting position (Count 4).

Girls from Real Secondary School, Valler, Norway, demonstrating exercises with Rhythm Balls

8. Back exercise bending forward

Sitting on the floor with stretched knees, leaning a little backward, right arm with the ball extended backward on the right side, left arm extended forward. Roll the ball forward on the right side (Count 1-4). Pass in front of the toes and change to left hand, back on the left side (Count 5-8). Repeat on left side.

9. Abdominal exercise

Sitting as 8. Arms extended to the sides, hands on the floor, the ball under the right hand. Lean the back backward, raise the legs with stretched knees and roll the ball under the legs to the left hand (Count 1) to starting position (Count 2). Repeat with left hand (Count 3-4).

10. Figure 8 movement

Standing with the feet together the ball in both hands, arms extended forward to the right side.

(a) Draw a figure 8 in front of the face. Relax and stretch the knees.

(b) Same as *a* the head and upper body follow the ball.

(c) As *b* the whole body follows the ball, relax the knees, push the hips to the side.

11. Skip

(a) Standing with the arms extended forward, the ball rests in both hands. Skip forward, raise the knees a little, stretch the ankles, small throw.

(b) As *a* 1-2-3-4-5-6, drop the ball to the floor and catch it. Do not stop, keep on skipping (Count 7-8).

(c) As *b* with a throw straight up, a little forward (Count 7). Catch the ball (Count 8).

PROGRAM II

1. **Skip**

   Standing with arms extended forward, eye-height, double shoulder distance between the hands, the ball in the right hand. Start with left foot, skip, forward, throw the ball with a low throw over the left hand, bend upper part and head to the left (Count 1). Repeat with right (Count 2). Not too slow, with good speed forward.

2. Standing with the feet together, arms extended to the sides, shoulder height, the ball in right hand. Throw and catch with right hand, rising high on toes and relaxing (1), repeat (2); on (3) change the ball behind the back to left hand, to starting position (4). Repeat with left hand (5-6-7-8).

3. Standing on the right foot, left leg extended to the side, the ball in the right hand. Throw as exercise 2. Standing on the right foot, raise leg a little to the side every time the ball moves up (1-2-3 Count), move the ball behind the back, bend both knees, push left hip to the side and move the weight over to the left foot, stretch up (Count 4). Repeat with left hand, standing on left foot (Count 5-6-7-8).

4. (a) Standing with feet together, arms extended to the sides shoulder-height, the ball in the right hand. Throw the ball under the left knee, *see Program I, Exercise 3*, catch the ball with the left hand, left foot down, feet together, throw the ball and rise on toes. (Count 1-2). The catch of the ball is the start to next throw and so on from side to side.

   (b) Same throw as *a*. Throw the ball in a bowline under and over the knee and catch with the same hand, bend to the side. Several times with right arm under left knee, repeat with left arm under right knee.

5. **Throw over the head**

   Standing on the right foot, left leg extended to the side, pointed toe on the floor, arms extended to the sides, shoulder-height, bend to the right side. Throw the ball over the head, rise on toes on both feet, catch the ball with the left hand and move the weight over to left foot, bend to the left. Throw with the side muscles, look at the ball.

6. **Jump**

   Standing with the ball in right hand, high hop on left foot, raise right knee while bouncing the ball with right hand, *hop* and then hop on right foot, raise left knee, *hop* and move forward. Practice also bouncing the ball with left hand.[11]

7. Bounce the ball with 2 hands

Standing with the feet together, arms extended forward, shoulder-height, the ball rests in both hands. Turn the hands and bounce the ball, relax knees and back (Count 1), stretch, move the arms a little up to the side in a circle (to either side) and catch the ball underneath, relax and stretch (Count 2).

8. Throw forward up with one hand

(a) Standing with the feet together, the ball in the right hand by the hip, left arm extended forward. Throw the ball with a good stretch up; the ball rolls to the fingers and up (Count 1). Catch the ball with right hand to starting position, relax knees and back (Count 2). Several times. Repeat with left hand.

(b) As *a* rise on toes on Count 1.

(c) As *b* 3 throws 1-2, 3-4, 5-6 throw higher over to the other hand 7-8. Repeat.

9. Lying prone

Lying on the stomach, arms extended to the sides, the ball under right hand on the floor. Roll the ball under the chest over to the left hand, raise head and shoulder, (Count 1) catch with left hand and relax (Count 2). Repeat (Count 3-4) and so on.

10. Lying supine

Lying on the back, the ball between the feet, arms extended upward on the floor. Move the legs (with the ball) up, give the ball over in the hand (Count 1-4), move the legs down to starting position (5-8) sit up stretch the arms (with the ball) up (1-2), bend forward and give the ball over to the feet (3-4) roll back to starting position with rounded back (5-7) arms extended up (8).

11. Standing with feet together, the ball in the right hand by the hip, left extended forward. Throw the ball forward up (Count 1). Catch the ball with the left hand, drop the left arm down backward, turn to the left (Count 2). Throw the ball in turned position and catch it (Count 3-4). Repeat from turned position (5-6-7-8).

------

[11]High skip — JN.

12. **Standing with the ball in both hands,** bend
    arms, chest high. Bend forward, stretch arms
    forward and throw the ball (Count 1). Catch
    the ball and relax neck, back and knees (Count
    2). Roll the back up, throw the ball straight up
    (Count 3). Catch the ball to starting position,
    relax knees and back (Count 4).

PROGRAM III

1. Waltz run

Standing, arms extended forward, head high, palms up, the ball lying in the hand. Run forward in waltz rhythm 1-2-3, 4-5-6. Relax arms and stretch forward, bend a little to the left when starting with left foot, the ball leaves the hands, a little throw forward up, 1-2-3, repeat bending to the right starting with right foot 4-5-6, etc. Good speed forward.

2. Throwing obliquely

(a) Standing on right foot, left foot extended to the side, pointed toe close to the floor, arms extended to the sides, shoulder high, the ball in right hand. Throw the ball, rise on tiptoe and raise left leg to the side, catch the ball, relax standing knee and the back, etc. Repeat standing on left foot, the ball on left hand. Waltz rhythm. (b) As *a* three times: 1-2-3, change the ball to left hand behind the back moving the weight to left foot 4. Repeat with left hand 1-2-3, change to right hand 4, etc.

3. With balance step

Standing on right foot, left leg extended forward, pointed toe, the ball in right hand by the hip, left arm extended forward. Throw the ball forward up, move the weight to front foot, raise the back leg a little, arch the upper back 1 (left arm swings down, backward, while the right arm swings forward for the throw). Catch the ball with right hand, right arm swinging down backward, left arm forward, move weight to back foot, relax back 2. Several times with right hand, repeat with the left.

4. Throw under stretched leg

Standing with arms extended to the sides, the ball in right hand. Move a short step forward with right foot, swing left leg forward, up, and throw the ball under left leg, to left hand 1 (the weight a little backward). Catch the ball with left hand, two steps on the spot (left, right) 2. (The weight a little forward.) Step forward on left foot, swing right leg forward, up, throw the ball under right leg to right hand, etc., 3-4.

5. Bodywave

Standing with arms extended forward shoulder high, the ball in right hand. Swing right arm down, backward, up with a bodywave 1, drop the ball to left hand, relax back and knees 2. Repeat with left arm, etc., 3-4.

6. Throw with turned arm, forward bending

Standing with right arm extended to the side, the ball in right hand. Swing the arm in a big circle upward, forward down, and turn the arm with palm up in the lowest position, bend at the same time forward with rounded back and bent knees. Throw the ball straight up, stretch back and knees (1). Catch the ball with the right hand, dipping your knees (2). Continue directly to next swing without any stop in starting position, several times with right arm. Repeat with the left.

7. Leaps in mazurka rhythm

Standing with arms extended forward up, a little to the sides, the ball in right hand, head high. One leaping-step forward on left foot, throw the ball up in a bowline to the left hand. (1), 2 running steps forward, right, left, catch the ball with left hand, bend upper part a little to the left (2-3), repeat starting with right foot (4-5-7), etc. First practice the throw standing, then the running without ball and finally put the two together.

8. Figure 8 swing

Standing with the ball in both hands, see Program I, Exercise 10, stand on the right foot, left leg extended to the side, pointed toes on the floor. Draw a figure 8 in front of the face. Move the weight over to both feet, bending the knees, push the left hip to the side, bend to the right, move the weight over to left foot and stretch up 1. The ball has now made a half figure 8. Repeat to the right and ball has made a full figure 8. Continue moving from side to side without stopping waltz rhythm.

9. Throw straight up with one hand

(a) Standing with the ball in right hand, resting on the shoulder, palm up, the elbow hanging straight down, finger tips pointing backward. Throw the ball straight up, stretch the whole body, catch the ball, relax back and knees *1 —* and *2* and   . Repeat with left hand.

(b) Same as *a*, rising on toes in each throw.

10. Throw under the arm

(a) Standing with right arm extended to the side, left arm extended forward, both shoulder high. The ball in right hand. Throw the ball in a bowline under, up and over left arm, bend to the right side (1), catch the ball with right hand, a small throw and stretch up (2).

(b) Same throw as *a*. When catching the ball on 2, rise on tiptoe and throw the ball higher. Repeat with left arm.

PROGRAM IV

1. Running in waltz rhythm

Standing, arms extended forward, the ball in right hand. 3 running steps forward 1-2-3, right arm (with the ball), swing down backward turn to the right, (look at the ball), a little throw. Three running steps forward and the right arm swings down, forward and throws the ball to the left hand 4-5-6. Repeat swinging left arm 1-2-3, 4-5-6.

2. Throw with small jumps

Standing on right foot, left leg extended to the side, right arm extended to the side, the ball in right hand. Throw the ball, hop three times 1-2-3, change the ball to left hand (4). Repeat with left arm, hopping on left foot (5-8).

3. Throw over the head, moving to the side

Weight on right foot, left leg extended to the side arms out sideward shoulder height, the ball in right hand. Throw the ball over the head to left hand (see Program II, exercise 5) one step to the left with left foot, pull right foot crossing in front with toes pointing to the right, rise on tiptoe (1-2), left foot step to the left, rise on tiptoe, a little throw with left hand and catch the ball (3-4). Repeat to the opposite side (5-8).

4. Throw with one hand, 90° turn

Standing, the arms extended to the sides, the ball in right hand. Swing right arm down, to the left, right foot one step to the left crossing in front, 90° turn to the left, throw the ball forward up while rising on tiptoe (see Program II, exercise 8b) (1). Catch the ball with right hand, 2 steps on the spot, left, right, turn 90° to starting position, change the ball behind the back to left hand (2). Repeat with left hand, turning to the right (3-4), etc.

5. Jumps

Standing with the arms extended to the sides, the ball in right hand. Leap to the left on left foot (1). 2 steps backward, right, left (2-3), leap to the right on right foot (4). 2 steps forward, left, right (5-6). The leaps and steps are building a circle, lean toward the center of the circle. The ball changes in front of the body on (1-3) — behind on (4-6), on jump on both feet, bounce the ball (1-3), catch the ball (4-6). Continue several times to the left. Repeat to the right. Later on: once to the left, once to the right, etc.

(a) Practice the leap first without the ball. Raise knees when leaping on 1, and 4.

(b) Practice the change of the ball from one hand to the other in front and back. Stress the hipwork (hips moving from side to side) *a + b*.

6. Backward bending

(a) Standing, the ball in the right hand by the hip. Swing both arms forward, relax and stretch knees and back (1), the right arm continues upward, bend right arm, the hand with the ball rests on the shoulder, palm up, bend the upper part backward (2), deeper bending in back and knees and stretch with right armswing up (3), the arm continues forward down, a little backward, bend upper part forward, rounded back, relaxed knees (4).

Turn the hand and swing forward up, etc. (5-8). Several times with right arm. Repeat with left arm......

(b) Same as *a*. Change the ball to the other hand behind the back on 4 and 8.

7. Forward bending

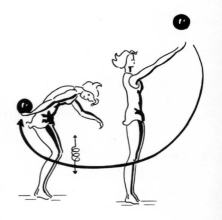

(a) Standing position as 6. Swing right arm forward up, throw the ball a little, stretch the whole body (1), catch the ball from above, swing the arm down, backward with relaxed bending forward (2). Turn the hand, swing the arm forward, up, etc. Several times with right arm. Repeat with the left.

(b) Same as a, rising on tiptoe on each "1."

(c) Same as *a*. Standing on right foot, left leg extended forward with stretched toes touching the floor. Move the weight to the front foot on (1), move the weight to the back foot with forward bending and relaxing on (2).

8. Throw from one hand to the other

(a) Standing on right foot, left leg extended to the side, stretched ankle, toes close to the floor, arms extended to the sides, the ball in right hand. Throw the ball in a bowline down and up to the left hand moving the weight over and sidebending as the figure 8 movement (1), to the other side (2). Continue from hand to hand without stop, waltz rhythm.

(b) Move the weight from foot to foot as a, roll the ball from hand to hand in front of the body (1), behind (2). Move the arms from side to side (from the shoulder).

(c) Combine a + b, exercise a, 4 times, then exercise b, 4 times.

9. Throw behind the back

(a) Standing, arms extended to the sides, the ball in right hand. Throw the ball behind the back from right hip up, over left shoulder, turn the upper part to the right, rounded back, relaxed knees, look over left shoulder (1). Stretch up and catch the ball with both hands and let it slide over in the right hand (2). Continue with right hand, nonstop. Repeat with left hand.

(b) Same as a. Catch the ball with the opposite hand, and do the exercise from side to side without stopping.

10. Throw under the arm

(a) Standing on right foot, left leg extended to the side, stretched ankle, toes touching the floor, right arm to the side, left arm extended forward, both shoulder high. Throw under, up, and over left arm, move the weight to left foot, bend to the right side (1). Catch the ball with right hand, move the weight to right foot rising on tiptoe, swing right arm to the side up, throw the ball, good stretch (2). Several times with right arm. Repeat with left arm.

(b) Same as a, twice, (1-2, 3-4). Throw the ball 3 times under, up and over left arm, the weight on left foot, dipping the knee (5-7). Throw a little higher and catch the ball with left hand, swinging the arm sideways up, while throwing the ball, rising on tiptoe (8). Repeat with left hand.

(c) Same as a and b with a small flexible jump instead of rising on tiptoe.

11. Polka

Standing with the arms extended forward, up, the ball in right hand. 2 running steps forward, left, right, — right arm swings down, a little backward (1-2), step forward on left foot and hop, right leg "hanging" relaxed behind, right arm swinging forward up, throwing the ball to the left hand, (3-4). Repeat with left arm, right foot starting (5-8), etc.

PROGRAM V

1. Throw over the head in turned position

(a) Standing, arms extended forward, shoulder high, the ball in right hand. Swing right arm down, backward, turn the upper part of the body to the right, relax and stretch knees (1). Throw the ball forward in a bowline over the head to left hand (2). Left arm then swings directly down backward, turning the upper body to the left (3). Throw over head to right hand, etc.

(b) Same as *a*, rise on tiptoe when throwing the ball over the head on 2 and 4, etc.

(c) Same exercise moving forward in waltz rhythm 1 (1-2-3), 2 (4-5-6), etc.

2. Throw to the side with side step

(a) Standing, arms extended forward, the ball in right hand. Swing right arm down, to the side, a little upward, take a step to the right, moving the weight over and rising on tiptoe, (1). Catch the ball with right hand, swing the arm down, forward with relaxed sidebending to the right, move the weight to left foot, pull right foot to the left, to starting position (2). The hip leads the movement, the ball slides over in left hand. Repeat to the left (3-4).

(b) Same as *a*, with jump on *1, 3*, etc.

8. Bodywave and bounce

Standing, arms extended forward, the ball in right hand. Right arm swings down, backward up in a big circle with bodywave (See Program II, Exercise 5) (1), bounce the ball on the floor, relax back and knees (2). Catch the ball on the top and start immediately new armswing with bodywave (3-4), etc.

4. Bending forward throw with turned arm

(See Program III, Exercise 6.) Standing, right arm extended to the side, keeping the ball. Swing right arm in a big circle up forward, down, turn the hand, palm up and throw the ball, bend forward with rounded back and bent knees, (1). Stretch up and catch the ball with right hand (2), repeat twice (3-4, 5-6), the fourth time throw the ball over the head to left hand (7-8).

5. Side exercise with jump

Standing with right arm extended to the side the ball in right hand. Swing right arm down, to the left crossing in front of the body, right foot step to the left, crossing in front with a small, flexible jump, raise left knee, turned 90° to the left. Bend upper part to the right (1). Right arm swings down, out, with a small throw, stretch left knee and put left foot on the floor in a jump, raise right leg to the side (2). Make the movement straight to the side. Keep moving to the left several times. Repeat to the right.

6. **Figure 8 swing moving the weight from side to side with both and one arm**

(See Program III, Exercise 8.) Start the figure 8 swing from the right to the left (1-2), etc. Little by little go over to swinging the ball with right hand. Continue the figure 8 movement changing the weight from side to side and keep the rhythm as before. Repeat swinging from left to right and continue with the left arm alone.

7. **Throw the ball with 180° turn**

(a) Repeat exercise 8, Program IV.

(b) Standing on right foot, right arm extended to the side, the ball in right hand, throw the ball down, up to left hand as *a*, move the weight to left foot, move right foot close to the left and turn 90° to the left (1), the left arm with the ball swings down, to the side, left footstep to the left, move the weight to left foot 90° turn to the left (2). (The performer has now turned 180° from starting position, standing on the left foot, left arm extended to the side, the ball in left hand.) Repeat with turn to the right (3-4), etc.

8. **Step forward diagonally with armswing and throw**

(a) Standing with the weight on left foot, arms extended to the sides, the ball in right hand. A short step with right foot forward to the left crossing in front bend your knees, raising left foot from the floor behind right leg, swing right arm forward to the left with a small throw (1), dipping right knee, stretch up, right arm swings down, sideways up, throwing the ball over the head to the left hand, at the same time 2 small steps on the spot, left, right (2-3). Repeat with left arm and foot (4-6), etc.

(b) Same exercise as *a*, with small flexible jumps on 1 and 2.

9. **Polka and jump with bouncing the ball**

(a) Polka See Program IV, Exercise 11.

(b) Hop raising your knee, bouncing the ball, see Program II, Exercise 6.

(a + b) Polka twice, 1-2-3-4, 5-6-7-8. 4 hops raising the knee 4 times, bouncing the ball with right hand on each jump, 1-2, 3-4, 5-6, 7-8, etc.

Mat Work and Tumbling

SECTION FIVE

MAT WORK AND TUMBLING

The following exercises are the tumbling on mats progressively from basic to more advanced exercise. It is very important to stress the execution of the basic exercises and make the students do them nearly perfectly before starting on the next step. To afford advanced exercises, they need the ability to know how to work with their heads down and they must be able to control the strength and flexibility in the different parts of the body and the extremities. When starting a new exercise, the best class organization is to have the students lined up on the long side of the mat in one, sometimes in two, or three lines (one performer, one or two spotters) and then divide in squads for free practice.

1. Elementary forward roll

(a) Sitting on the side of the mat, back to the mat, knees bent, feet on floor, head tucked, rounded back, arms grasping the knees. Rock back, up on the neck, and forth to starting position, several times to feel the rounded back.

(b) As *a* in squat position, rock back and forth several times.

(c) Squat position, facing the mat, hands on the mat, shoulders distance apart, chin to chest. Lean forward, bending the arms and pushing with the feet, roll over. Landing on neck and shoulders, up to starting position.

(d) Little by little two or more rolls in a row, finish with a high jump arms extended upward, look up.

(e) Finish with a jump and 180° turn as with *d*, down to starting position, ready to a new forward roll, arms moving forward up, forward down.

Diving forward roll

(a) Squat position, arms extended in front of the body, chin tucked in, finger tips on the mat. Roll forward, stretching your knees, bend the knees quickly in the last moment and place feet on the mat. Up to starting position.

(b) Squat position, arms extended forward, shoulder high. Push with the feet and dive a little, land with hands on the mat from above and roll over as *a*.

(c) Starting position as *b*. Push more with the feet and little by little, make the roll higher and longer.

Spotting

The spotter standing on her knees beside the performer, one hand on backhead-neck, one grasping the ankle to help rolling.

2. Backward roll

(a) Repeat the rocking back and forth as for starting forward roll, but this time keep the hands above the shoulders, palms up, fingers pointing backward, thumbs pointing to the ears.

(b) Rock back and forth as *a*, twice, then the third time go all the way over. Place hands on the mat and push. Get up to starting position.

(c) As *a*, with legs extended backward down, bend your knees while the toes touch the mat and the arms start pushing.

(d) Several backward rolls in a row, finish with a high jump.

(e) Combine one forward roll, jump and turn 180° down to squat position and directly backward roll.

See Spotting.

If any student has difficulties in making the backward roll, help her like this: The performer rolls relaxed backward up on the neck, place hands on the mat under shoulders, palms on the mat. The spotter standing in line with shoulders of performer, grasps the hips and pulls her over; *do not push.*

3. Headstand (with bent knees)

(a) Standing on the knees, hands on the mat shoulder width apart, put the forehead on the mat in front of the hands (head and hands form a tripod). Stretch knees and slide the weight over to head and hands, bend your knees and stand on head (with knees bent).

(b) Start the headstand as *a*, stretch knees and hips.

(c) Starting position as *a*, lift legs to headstand with stretched knees.

(d) Headstand forward roll. When standing on the head, bend the neck, chin to chest, round the back and roll over.

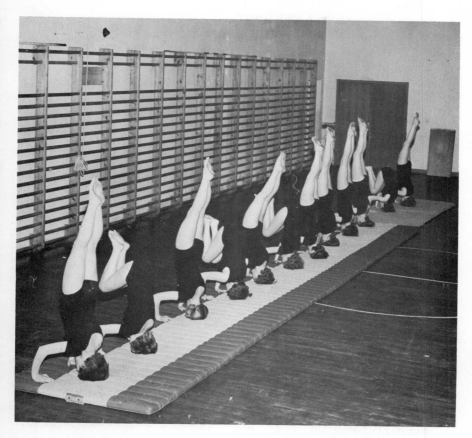

Girls from Real Secondary School, Valler, Norway, demonstrating Headstand with bent and stretched knees

Spotting

Always work 2 and 2 together, one standing on the side with one arm behind the back of the performer to avoid her falling over on flat back. When spotting the headstand forward roll, control the headstand first, then go in front of the performer and grasp her ankles, let her roll slowly down on the neck and rounded back. Keep the legs stretched to the last moment, bend knees quickly, place feet on the mat and come to squat position.

4. Handstand

To get used to keeping the weight on the arms and to get the hips up, start with:

Hare-jump

(a) Squat position, arms extended forward shoulder high, shoulder distance apart. Place hands on the floor, shoulder distance apart, rock forward, the hands balancing the weight, knees and hips tucked, elbows straight, head up, hips vertically above the head. Land smoothly in starting position on the toes. Count: Up! — and down!

(b) Hare-jumps moving forward and backward.

(c) Hare-jumps on the spot with stretched knees.

Girls from Real Secondary School, Valler, Norway, demonstrating Hare Jumps

Handstands against the wall.

(a) Place hands approximately 1/2 yard from the wall, shoulder distance between the hands, fingers spread and slightly bent, shoulders a little forward, look about one foot forward on the floor, weight on

Girls from Real Secondary School, Valler, Norway, demonstrating Handstands against the wall

the hands, one leg extended backward, hips high. Kick the back leg, "swingleg," over the head, get the hips up, touch the wall, the "take-off" leg hanging relaxed extended, down to starting position. Up! — and — down!

(b) Start as *a*. When the performer gets the back straight up and has the balance touching the wall, raise the "take-off" leg, stretch up as much as possible, tighten abdominal, hip, and gluteal muscles. Down to starting position with

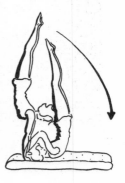

1. one leg at a time
2. both legs and knees flexed
3. stretched legs, hips flexed

(c) Handstands forward roll. Spotting as head-stand forward roll.

Handstand, free on floor

Work in pairs. Progression, same as handstand against wall. Avoid falling over. If the weight is moving too far over, bend or lift one arm and the performer will turn and get down on her feet.

Girl from Real Secondary School, Valler Norway, demonstrating Handstand free on floor

Seventeen year old girl from Real Secondary School, Valler, Norway, demonstrating Handstand Forward Roll

Spotting

Let the students practice by themselves as much as possible. However, if anybody has difficulties in getting up, or is afraid to keep the weight on her arms, she needs spotting.

(a) Spotter stands back against the wall, legs separated, right knee slightly bent. Tumbler places one hand on either side of her right foot, leans left shoulder against her knee and stands in the starting position. The spotter catches the tumbler's hips and helps her to get up.

Girls from Real Secondary School, Valler, Norway, demonstrating Handstand with stretched knees, flexed hips. From this position stretch to handstand. obs: The spotting

(b) Two spotters standing on one knee on each side of the performer, foot on floor close to the wall, knee bent, one hand under the tumbler's shoulder; the other hand under the performer's hips, helping her up; the performer's arms resting against the spotter's knees.

(c) One spotter on the side as in *b*.

5. Cartwheel

Class organization: The class lined up along one side of the gym — work across to the other side following a single chalked line. Later on work in pairs correcting each other.

Starting position:

Standing on a line, tumbler faces direction of the movement (doing cartwheel to the right) keep right knee bent in front of the body, the weight on left foot, right arm extended forward, left arm extended straight up.

(a) Lean forward, place right foot, then right hand on the line, in front of the foot, fingers pointing 90° to the right, put left hand on the line in front of the right one about shoulder distance apart, fingers pointing 90° to the right. Move the weight over the arms, kick hips up, over the head with bent knees, land on the line. Count: hand — hand — foot — foot. (1-2-3-4, even rhythm).

(b) Little by little increase the speed and stretch the legs. Stress to get both hands and feet on one line.

Girls from Real Secondary School, Valler, Norway, demonstrating Cartwheel

(c) Move left hand farther forward, increase the speed forward, push with standing foot.

(d) Push with the last hand, land on the toes, relaxed knee and ankle, to standing position with the arms extended to the sides. Always practice the cartwheel to both sides from the beginning.

Running cartwheel to the best side

(a) The "take-off." Cartwheel to the right side. Standing on right foot left leg extended backward, arms a little backward. Step forward on left foot with a jump, raise right knee and the arms to starting position for cartwheel (1), step forward on right foot and lower the arms to starting position (2). Continue and count: jump! — and step, jump! and step.

(b) The take-off and cartwheel.

(c) 3 steps forward, take-off and cartwheel.

(d) 5 or more steps, full run and cartwheel.
Having done the running cartwheel, turn 90° and continue running forward.

(e) Cartwheel on one hand.

6. Headspring

Class organization: The students working in pairs lined up along the side of the long mat.

(a) Place hands and head on the mat for headstands; the spotter standing behind the tumbler and catching the hips. Push with both legs and move the weight over so that the back makes approximately an angle of 30° with the perpendicular line, down to starting position. Count: Up! — and down! Up! — and down. Obs.! Stand on the forehead.

(b) Mats lined up against the wall, the students working in pairs. Place head about one foot from the wall to the same starting position as *a*, the spotters standing by the side. Move weight over to the hips, touch the wall. The spotter places one hand on the lower back, one hand on the upper leg and helps the tumbler to stretch the hips with a fast snap. Little by little, let the tumbler do it without help, only watch her.

(c) Class organization as *a*. Starting position as *a*. When the weight is moved over, stretch the hip with a fast snap as *b* stretch the arms

Girls from Real Secondary School, Valler, Norway, demonstrating Headspring a

Girls from Real Secondary School, Valler, Norway, demonstrating Headspring c

to a handstand, leaning over on the spotter's shoulder. The spotter helps to get up. Count: and — up!

(d) Use the rolled mat at one end, 2 spotters straddle the mat on each side, keep one hand under the performer's shoulder, one hand on the lower back to give support and help lifting up. If necessary, use a third spotter grasping the ankles to help get the right angle before the snap and stretching. Little by little do the exercise with no or little help.

Girls from Real Secondary School, Valler, Norway, demonstrating Headspring d

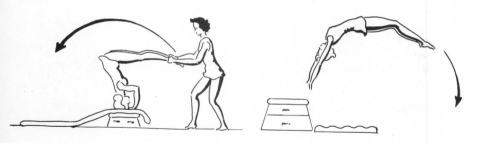

(e) As *d* on a plain mat with 2 spotters.

(f) As *e* with 1 spotter.

(g) As *d* doing the exercise alone and several times in a row (tempi-headspring).

7. Back extension

Class organization: The students lined up along the side of the long mat, sitting with the back to the mat, bent forward, straight legs.

(a) Roll backward up on the neck, place the hands under the shoulder as when doing the backward roll, stretch hip with a fast snap, roll down to starting position. Count: roll — stretch! — down. Continue several times.

Girls from Real Secondary School, Valler, Norway, demonstrating Back Extension a

(b) As *a* twice, third time stretch arms to full extension, pass the handstand position and land on the feet.

(c) While passing the handstand position push with the arms and snap the legs down from the hips so that the whole body will be off the mat. Finish in standing position. Spotting: two spotters on either side might help getting to handstands by grasping the performer's ankles on her way up, helping her to stretch by lifting her up.

Kip

Class organization. 3 students working together along the side of the long mat.

(a) The tumbler lying on the back, on the mat, legs and arms extended upward: one spotter on each side grasps one hand, holding each other round the wrist. Roll backward, up on the neck, legs approximately parallel with the mat. Move legs farther over, then up with a snap, stretching the hips and arching the back, land on the feet. The spotters holding one hand each, pull to help her.

(b) Starting position as *a* with the hands under shoulders as for making a backward roll. The spotters kneeling on each side of the tumbler lift upward and forward with one hand under the tumbler's shoulder, and the other under the hips as the tumbler snaps up.

(c) The kip without or with little support.
Obs. At the moment of snapping, the tumbler pushes off the mat with hands and back of the head and continues the whip of the legs until the body lands in squat position on the feet.

(d) As *c* with the hands above the knees, pushing off with the head only (snap-up).

8. Round off

Class organization: Students working in pairs lined up along the side of the long mat. The spotter is standing by the side in front of the tumbler.

(a) The tumbler standing in starting position for cartwheel, makes half a cartwheel, brings her legs together on top of the cartwheel to handstand position with 90° turn, flex the hips and push with the hands, landing on both feet with flexed ankles facing starting position. The spotter g r a s p s around the hips and helps lifting up.

(b) As *a* without any help.

(c) As *b* with one step, take-off, as for running cartwheel.

(d) With 3 or more steps.

(e) Round off with full speed.

OBS! Stretch arms forward down towards the mat, bend the upper part forward. The hands only touch the mat, use wrists and shoulders.

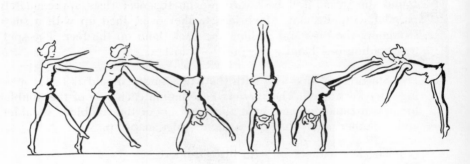

9. Handspring

Class organization. Students working in pairs lined up 3-4 yards from the wall. Spotter standing by the wall.

(a) One step, take off, place the hands far forward and do the handstand. Close the feet before getting all the way up, stretch the hips with a fast snap and touch the wall with both feet as high up on the wall as possible. The spotter helps with one hand under the performer's shoulder, the other on her hip.

(b) Class organization: Divide into squads. Use 2 benches and the little, upper part of the vaulting box. If benches and boxtops are not available use the rolled mat at one end. Spotters straddling on each side of the box helping the tumbler by holding under her shoulders and hips (to avoid her falling backward).

The tumbler stands on the farthest end of the benches, takes one step, skips and does the same as explained in *a*. She has no wall to stop her and therefore lands on her feet on the mat with flexed knees and ankles. When doing the snap, push with the hands to get high up, arch the back and keep head up.

Girls from Real Secondary School, Valler, Norway, demonstrating Handspring Landing on one foot at a time. The pictures are taken in 3 different periods of the Handspring. (13 different Handsprings)

(c) As *b* on plain mat with 2 spotters. Take a short run, skip and place hands as far forward as possible.

(d) Full speed with one or without spotter.
OBS! Keep the elbows straight, look forward, use wrist and shoulders to get the whole body off the mat. Place hands shoulder distance apart.

Balance Beam

SECTION SIX

BALANCE BEAM

The following exercises are some details used in the balance beam routines from the basic to the more advanced. Mostly all free floor exercises and jumps can be done on the balance beam. To get "full house" in the routine for national and international competitions, the performer has to have at least 5 "difficulties" in her program. The routine must be done continuously, without stopping, to keep up the balance and continuity. Start on a low beam and little by little make the beam higher.

MOUNTING THE BEAM

1. **At the end of the beam** (use take-off board)

   (a) Short run — take-off with both feet — on the beam in squat position, on one foot. Both hands on the beam — leaving the beam before the foot lands. The other leg hanging down. Rise fast to standing position. — Spotters stand on either side.

   (b) Short run — take-off with one foot — the other takes the beam in a long high step. The performer can either jump up in squat position with one leg extended forward (not touching the beam) or directly to standing position on one foot.

   (c) Run — take-off with both feet — jump directly to forward roll. OBS! The hands on top of the beam when starting the roll, change to catching under the beam, keep the elbows close. (Spotters on both sides can help tuck head — support shoulders first few times.)

   (d) Run and take-off as (c), jump directly to headstands, continue with a forward roll.

2. **Jumping on the side of the beam** (use take-off board)

   (a) Short run, take-off with both feet, jump to squat position on the beam.

   (b) Run and take-off as 1. Jump up on one knee, turning 90° to balance stand on one knee crosswise on the beam. (knee scale)

   (c) Run and take-off as 1. Jump up to straddle stand (feet wide apart).

   (d) Run in 30° angle with the beam, the take-off board in 30° angle with the beam, take-off with both feet, jump directly to shoulder stand with head on the opposite side of the beam. (Spotter stands on opposite side of beam in direct line with performer.)

ADVANCED DISMOUNTS

1. At the end of the beam

(a) Cartwheel from different positions, balance stand, squat position on one foot, the other leg extended backward, front foot on the beam,

Girl from Real Secondary School, Valler, Norway, demonstrating Cartwheel from the end of the beam

etc. OBS! When passing handstands, keep the legs together and land on both feet, push with the last hand.

(b) Round off: Start as with cartwheel. When passing handstand, turn 90° and land on the mat facing the end of the beam.

Girl from Real Secondary School, Valler, Norway, demonstrating Round-off from the end of the beam

(c) *Handspring*

(On first few attempts of foregoing 3 dismounts place one end of long mat over edge of beam. Spotter stands at side of beam facing performer's back.)

2. On the side of the beam

(a) Handstand arch over, land on both feet. Make the handstand from different positions as a 1/2 cartwheel.

(b) Handstand, turn 90° on one hand, swing the other arm down, to the side, land on the mat with the side to the beam. OBS! Dont bend the hips, raise upper part and land with the body straight, slightly bending the knees.

(Students should be able to perform these on floor first.)

Girl from Real Secondary School, Valler, Norway, demonstrating dismount from side of the beam (b, 1 and 2)

SKILLED EXERCISES "ADVANCED"

1. Forward roll

(a) "Creeping" forward roll. Start in squat position on one foot, the other leg extended backward, the front of foot resting on the beam. Tuck head, raise hips, roll over and change hands, catching under the beam, keep elbows close — lying on the back, legs extended upward.

(b) *Diving forward roll*

From squat position, arms extended forward shoulder high — ending in the same lying position as 1.

(c) Diving forward roll from different other positions, e.g., balance stand.

2. Backward roll

(a) Lying with the head on the side of the beam, one hand over (on the same side as the head), the other hand under the beam. Raise both legs roll over to kneestand on one knee, change the grip to both hands on the beam.

Fourteen year old student Real Secondary School, Valler, Norway, demonstrates Backward Roll with the head on the side of the beam

(b) Lying with the head *on* the beam. Roll over as 1, push with the hands on the beam, get up to squat position on one foot, the other leg hanging down — or in lunge position.

Student from Real Secondary School, Valler, Norway, demonstrates Backward Roll with head on the beam

3. Headstand

(a) Headstand from squat position, moving up with knees bent.

(b) As 1, moving up with one stretched leg at a time.

Sixteen year old girl from Real Secondary School, Valler, Norway, demonstrating Headstand on balance beam

(c) As 1 moving up with stretched knees (pike).

(d) Headstands from other positions, e.g., balance stand, one leg at a time.

Students from Real Secondary School, Valler, Norway, demonstrates balance stands on beam

(e) Headstand, forward roll, tuck the head in, roll fast over to lying position, legs extended upward, change the hands catching under the beam, elbows close. OBS! Doing the headstand on the beam, keep the elbows close.

4. Shoulderstand

Lying on the back with head on the side of the beam. (Position for backward roll.) Start as backward roll, when getting up on the shoulder, stretch hips and back and stand straight up on the shoulder. Continue rolling backward, bending the hips.

Student from Real Secondary School, Valler, Norway, demonstrates Shoulder Stand

5. Handstands

Handstands, forward roll. Get up in handstand position, roll over as headstand, forward roll.

(On foregoing five stunts spotter stands at side, supporting upper arm of performer.)

JUMPS

1. Moving forward

(a) A high, long leaping step forward.

(b) Jumping forward lifting alternately left and right knee to an angle of 90°.

(c) Scissors-jump.

2. On the spot

(a) "Split-jump," one forward, the other backward.

(b) Standing with one foot in front of the other, high jump, changing feet.

(c) Standing, high jump, bending your knees, heels close to the thigh.

TURNS

1. Standing, swing one leg forward up, rise on tiptoe on standing foot and turn 180°.

2. Standing, swing one leg backward, rise on tiptoe on standing foot and turn 180°.

3. Squat position with one leg extended forward the foot on the beam. Move the weight over to the front foot, swing the back leg in a horizontal circle forward, around with 180° turn, put the foot on the beam and continue the turn another 180°.

Vaultings on Buck, Horse, and Vaulting Box

SECTION SEVEN

VAULTINGS ON BUCK, HORSE, AND VAULTING BOX

1. **Buck (lengthwise)**

Straddle vault.

Students from Real Secondary School, Valler, Norway, demonstrate Straddle Vault over high buck. (lengthwise)

2. **Buck (crosswise)**

   (a) Straddle vault.

   (b) Jump over in squat position.

   (c) Jump over swinging both legs horizontally to one side (flank vault). Both hands on the buck in front of the body, if swinging the legs to the left, only touch the buck with left hand, move the weight over to right hand, lean to the right, swing left arm to the side, stretch the hips and land on the mat with the back to the buck. Practice both sides.

3. **Vaulting box or horse (crosswise)**

(a) Jump over in squat position. Extend legs after clearing box.

(b) Flank vault over swinging both legs to one side. See Buck, crosswise *c*.

(c) Rear vault. Start the jump as *b*. When passing the box, turn the back to it swinging your legs high. Pass the box in balance seat position. When swinging legs to the left, put left hand fast on the box behind left hip. Land on the mat with left side to the vaulting box. Practice both sides.

(d) As *a*. Move the springboard farther away from the box. After the take-off, swing legs and hips high up backward, land on stretched arms, push with the hands, bend the hips, and swing legs over with stretched knees, legs together. (Stoop vault.)

(e) As *d*. Straddle vault.

(f) *Headspring.*

Short run, take-off, land on your hands, bend the arms and place the forehead on the box, hips high and bent. Stretch hips with a

Students from Real Secondary School, Valler, Norway, demonstrate Headspring on Vaulting Box

fast snap and stretch the arms, push with the hands. (See tumbling, headspring.)

(g) *Handspring*

1) Medium high box, springboard approximately 1 1/2 feet from the box. Medium long run, good speed, energetic take-off, jump up, land on handstand with stretched arms on the box, arch over and push with the hands.

2) Make the vaultingbox (or sidehorse) higher and place the springboard, little by little, farther from the box. In the beginning, it will be easier to get up to handstand with hips slightly bent, then stretch out. Practice the last part of the handspring sepa-

Students from Real Secondary School, Valler, Norway, demonstrate Handspring on Vaulting Box

rately. Use the box crosswise, do the handstand on the end of the box and arch over, back very little arched, push with the hands. Perfect handspring is done with straight body (horizontal to floor or in lay-out) from the take-off, high and airy.

(h) *Cartwheel*

Run and take-off as g (handspring). After the take-off, turn 90° to the left (right), place the hands with fingers pointing to the left (right), do a cartwheel with the legs together, land on the mat with the side to the vaulting box.

4. Vaulting box in 30 — 45° with the running direction

(a) Start with outside foot, three steps take-off with outside foot, place innerside hand on the box, swing innerside leg high up, bend hip, swing the other leg fast up, pass the box in balance seat position,

Student from Real Secondary School, Valler, Norway, demonstrates exercise on Vaulting Box in 30°—45° angle

hips high over the box, push with the hand. Place the other hand on the box behind outside hip — land on the opposite side on both feet, side to the box. Practice both sides.

(b) Jump as *a*. When passing over the box, turn the body 180° on the innerside hand, stretch out the hips and land facing the opposite way. Springboard can be used in both *a* and *b*, however, it is more common to do it without.

5. Vaulting box (lengthwise)

(a) Cartwheel. Low vaulting box, springboard. Short run, take-off on one foot, regular cartwheel landing on one foot at a time.

(b) Jump over in squat position. Long run, energetic take-off, swing legs and hips high up backward, hand on the farthest end of the box,

Students at Real Secondary School, Valler, Norway, demonstrate exercise on Vaulting Box (lengthwise)

stretched arms, push with the hand, bend hips and knees and pass the box in squat position.

(c) As *b*, straddle vault.

(d) As *b*, bending the hips and passing the box with stretched knees.